## The Daily Catch about BrainFishing

Well, here it is, a guide that will put HR professionals out of business. No longer will front-line supervisors knock on my door for advice... once they read this book, they won't need me. The style shift outlined in **BrainFishing** speaks volumes about successful relationships in the workplace. The 18 questions near the end resonated most for me; it gave me better ways to convey ideas and generate solutions. Thanks for this!

— Leanne Gray, HBSc, CHRL
Director, Human Resources, Trillium Gift of Life Network

Do not underestimate this book! While the writing is whimsical and the message is simple, **BrainFishing** contains a treasure trove of practical and effective tips for improving the quality of our interactions with each other. It is an excellent addition to the field of conflict resolution, and for those committed to helping others resolve issues collaboratively. We would all be wise to put the book's lessons to work, and go fishing!

— Leslie H. Macleod B.A., LL.B., LL.M. (ADR)
Co-Director of LL.M. in Dispute Resolution Program
Osgoode Hall Law School, York University
Principal of Leslie H. Macleod & Associates

In a fun and practical way, the authors reinforce the value of well-placed and worded questions. The two colourful brains create playful references to help the reader retain and use the tools. At the same time, it could be used by negotiators to add value to any set of negotiations.

— Deborah M. Howes, LLB, ACCI, FCCI, CTAJ, C.Arb., C. Med.
IMI Cert. High Clouds Incorporated

In my over four decades of working in the fields of conflict resolution and negotiations I've witnessed far too many failed efforts. In **BrainFishing** the authors show you how the skilful use of questioning creates the type of communications, engagement, and free flow of information that is so vital to producing successful outcomes in problem solving, conflict and negotiations situations. They take you on the only fishing trip you'll ever go on where the results are guaranteed!

— Allen Orth
Former AVP Human Resources Queen's University
President, Concordia Consulting

This humorous and conversational pocketbook illustrates that good questions are at the heart of good solutions to problems. The imagery of engaging brains to "come out and play" and being able to find solutions while "spending a quiet day on the water" drew me to dive in and begin practicing right away. It will do the same for you!

— Susan Ruffo
Canadian Union of Public Employees, Manager and Educator (Retired)

**Brain Fishing** is a practical guide to training our minds in activating the Blue (problem solving) Brain to effectively engage others in finding solutions. It uses real examples of good questioning skills and storytelling to make this an effective "how to" guide. With practice, this can become our natural response to reach interest based solutions to problems in all aspects of our professional and personal lives. This book is meant to be shared and reflected upon. "Gone Fishin'" has taken on a whole new meaning!

— Paul Antaya
Superintendent of Human Resources
Greater Essex County District School Board

A Practice Guide to Questioning Skills

# BrainFishing

Stronger Relationships. Better Problem Solving.
And a bit of Neuroscience, too.

## GARY T. FURLONG & JIM HARRISON

www.brainfishing.ca

FriesenPress Publishing
Suite 300 – 990 Fort Street
Victoria, BC, V8V 3K2
Canada

www.friesenpress.com

ISBN
978-1-5255-3437-9 (Hardcover)
978-1-5255-3438-6 (Paperback)
978-1-5255-3439-3 (eBook)

*1.* bisac *code 001* – Business & Economics, Decision-Making & Problem Solving

Distributed to the trade by The Ingram Book Company

Printed by Marquis  MARQUIS

# Contents

# Acknowledgements

We never go fishing alone. We want to acknowledge some of the many people who made this, and so much more, possible:

## Gary T. Furlong

The entire Agree Dispute Resolution family, who put up with my questions and so much more.

Jim Camp, a true master of powerful questions and an exceptional teacher and mentor.

My colleagues Josh and Ken at the Sports Conflict Institute, where this work truly is a sport.

Callan, Tess, and Ronalda – my foundation, and forever my test subjects.

## Jim Harrison

My colleagues at Stackhouse Garber Associates, Optime International and The Covenant Group who helped me explore and refine my questioning skills.

Peter Pichler, a client who became a close friend and gave me unlimited opportunities to expand my understanding of business and the world.

My wife, Arlene, and my four amazing children, Ali, Koal, Jack and Maisie, all of whom I love without question.

And finally, my late sister Christine Harrison, who taught me to take thinking seriously and to follow my instincts to question everything. I miss her very much.

# Hunting vs. Fishing

This is a Practice Guide and a pocket book. It's a simple map to making your relationships, conversations, and interactions dramatically easier and more effective. That's it, and no more.

The Guide's title, let's face it, is silly. It is a whimsical metaphor designed to get your attention. But it also points to the crux of the book and should help you decide whether this Practice Guide will help you or not. After the Introduction, we'll limit the use of metaphors, we promise. But here, in the Introduction, we'll not only use a Big Metaphor to make a serious point about the skills this book offers, we'll extend it way past silly. Just for fun. Here goes.

Problem solving, negotiating, managing, selling and resolving conflict all have these things in common – interacting, working, and communicating with other people. Our lives, both personal and professional, are filled with working and communicating with others.

In many of these exchanges we are trying to deal with a problem or an issue of some kind, trying to find a better solution or answer, one that we can live with and that the other person will agree to. Day in and day out, dealing with issues and problems, large or small, takes up a huge percentage of our waking time. We are regularly faced with working out issues with the people around us. As a rough estimate, if we average five of these issues per day, five small or medium-sized problems that we need to resolve or address with other people, it works out to about 150 every month. Imagine if just half of these were resolved *faster*, *easier*, and *better* – and with way less friction or stress. Now imagine if *most* of them were. Interested? That's what this Practice Guide is about.

Here's where the Big Metaphor starts. There are typically two ways people try and solve problems with other people. First, some people see themselves as hunters. They stalk through the forest, rifle in hand, and when they see something they want from someone, they go directly after it – they "shoot". In this silly metaphor, they target what they want, they push their ideas on others, they argue, they cajole, they pressure, they beg, they bully. They aggressively go after their goal until the other person gives in to them. And often, when they "bag" the result they were looking for, they leave the other person – their "prey" – just happy it's over, and not much else. If the other party fights back, however, it can turn into a metaphorical shootout – both people pushing, resisting, fighting, arguing to a standstill, until one or both walk (or run) away – with everybody wounded.

Secondly, if the prey doesn't want to fight like this, they simply get outta Dodge – they behave like smart prey often does, and make themselves scarce. They avoid, they ignore, or worse, they say "yes" just to end the ordeal and then slip away as quickly as possible, often nursing serious resentment.

In both cases, whether hunter or prey, the outcome is lousy for somebody, and often for everybody. Many a hunter has spent a few miserable days in the woods, cold and wet, returning home empty handed. Hunting, in this metaphor, kind of sucks. Sure, the times when the hunter bags some prey, there is much happiness – until next time, when the cold and wet beckons again and many a hunter chooses to stay home, thinking that a little bit of hunger ain't all that bad when compared to the alternative. There was a time – in the real world – when we had to hunt to stay alive. But that time, for most of us, is long gone. So we think hunting – specifically as a way of solving problems – should go that route as well.

This Practice Guide is about another way, a different approach to successfully working with other people, one that always sends you home with a "catch", i.e. with a constructive and positive outcome for everyone. There is another, and better, metaphor than hunters and prey.

That metaphor is fishing. More specifically – **BrainFishing**.

Fishing is the metaphorical opposite of hunting in many ways. Instead of tracking, stalking, and then shooting the other person, fishing is about catching their attention, hooking their interest, luring them into a real dialogue where everyone gets what they need (well, okay, maybe not the real-life fish – but remember, this is a *metaphor*). It's about using some of the most powerful bait there is – the possibility that interacting and working with you will get them *what they need and what they want* without being threatened, without being hunted or stalked.

BrainFishing, to be clear, is not the same as sport fishing for trophies to put on your wall at home (hey, no metaphor is perfect). BrainFishing is fishing with only one goal – to catch that other brain's interest, to guide them into a quiet pool or eddy where you can solve a problem *together*. In this way, BrainFishing is more like barbless fishing, where once you catch their attention, you release them to be part of the solution. It's the best form of "catch and release" there is.

BrainFishing is a simpler way to engage with everyone, one that feels more like a quiet day on the water enjoying the sun as you solve problems. Compare that to trudging through the woods, cold and wet, trying to force everyone into a solution that works for you but not for them. Most of us, I think, would prefer a quiet day of fishing!

This approach, of course, is not limited to quiet days sitting in the sun. Since so much of our time is spent interacting with other people, BrainFishing can be applied just about everywhere. The skills in this Practice Guide are the essential skills needed to succeed whenever we are working with other people. These skills and tools can improve our leadership of teams, help negotiate contracts, repair relationships with clients, with colleagues, with suppliers, even manage the performance of our employees. The list goes on: BrainFishing can be productively applied to sales, to operations, to coaching, even to talking with our children, our partners, and our family members. Problems arise in all parts of life, and better problem solving will help us everywhere. Our examples and "fish stories" throughout the Practice Guide will look at many of these situations.

Finally, the information in this book has strong support from much of the research being done in neuroscience and psychology on how the brain and the mind operate. Current research shows that the skills, tools and approaches used by BrainFishing are informed by many of its findings, and these findings contribute to an understanding of why the BrainFishing approach can be effective and successful. We've confined most of that background to the final chapter, Chapter Three. We want the primary focus of this guide to be on learning the skills and tools; we don't want to get you mired down in the technical details, just like we wouldn't want you to spend all day learning the complex reasons why a boat floats on water before getting out on the lake. The BrainFishing approach works; the reasons why it works are also important and are outlined in the last chapter for those of you who are interested.

This little book, then, is all about BrainFishing. As described, this is a Practice Guide, and therefore we have kept it short and to the point. There are only three chapters, followed by a summary of the skills and tools and a set of worksheets to take away, organized like this:

- **Chapter One** is the "**Why**". It's about the shift in behaviour that characterizes BrainFishing – and why it's the best approach to change just about every interaction with other people in your life.

- **Chapter Two** is the "**What**" and the "**How**". It's about the art and science of questioning skills, along with a series of cases all taken from real life – with names and details changed for privacy. These cases demonstrate the BrainFishing approach and the shift from hunting to BrainFishing. This chapter will also give you a full set of equipment, your own personal "tackle box" filled with the tools and skills you'll need for BrainFishing.

- **Chapter Three**, as we said, is the **background** and the **research**. We know that some of you are skeptics, doubters, or even just strongly analytical. We respect that, so we've included the science that this is based on – the deeper "Why". We'll give you the short version on current research in neurobiology, psychology, and other writings that support what we're talking about, as well as tips for better BrainFishing.

- **The BrainFishing Tackle Box**, which is a **summary** of all the useful bits from the book.
- **BrainFishing Worksheets**, for you to **practice** to your heart's content.

That's it for the BrainFishing metaphor – for now. If you find yourself struggling with the imagery of hunting and fishing, we apologize. We found it to be the most direct way to convey in simple and engaging terms the critical shift from domination to engagement as a skill set for success. So hang in there. We think you'll find the information in this Guide is well worth the metaphor.

So, if the opportunity for better relationships, deeper engagement, and better problem-solving outcomes entices you, come on along with us. Hang up that "Gone Fishin'" sign for a while, and see what you think.

# Fishing For Brains

*Or: "What the heck are we talking about?*
*BrainFishing? Are you kidding?"*

Yeah, sort of kidding. We did try to trademark the term, but felt so stupid at the lawyer's office that we walked.

What we're dead serious about is the shift from metaphorical hunting, to metaphorical fishing. Here's what we mean.

## Hunting is Telling

The single most common way we communicate and engage with each other is through "telling". We talk *at* people. Spitting out words or phrases aimed at others. Targeting them with our brilliant thoughts. Explaining ad nauseum. Communication, to most people, means conveying information, giving others the gift of our thoughts, our reasons, our rationale. In other words – some version of *telling*. I tell you about my project, I tell you why it's important, I tell you what I need from you, tell you why your idea won't work, tell you I like you, tell you I don't like you, etc. Here's how that kind of telling usually makes people react:

- I tell you about my project (*Yawn*)
- I tell you why it's important (*Who cares?*)
- I tell you what I need from you (*I'm busy*)
- I tell you why your idea won't work (*Yours won't work either*)
- I tell you I like you (*That's just flattery and BS*)
- I tell you I don't like you (*Well, I don't like you either!*)

You can see the pattern. When we tell, when we assert something, it somehow causes the other party to take the opposite point of view.

Newton identified this principle back in the 1600's, while inventing physics. Newton's Third Law of Motion states that:

**"For every Action, there is an Equal, and _Opposite_, Reaction."**

Phrased in the BrainFishing way, it might sound like this:

**"For every Tell, there is an Equal, and _Opposite_, Tell."**

In other words, if I assert that something is true, you tend to focus on and tell me the reasons it may _not_ be true. If I tell you why my idea is good, you tend to see the ways it might _not_ be so good. Even if I assert something you _know_ to be 98% true, what do you focus on in your response? Most likely, it's the 2%. So telling, in and of itself, draws an opposing argument – almost automatically (kind of like physics, right?).

The net result is this: When I tell, I tend to make my own job harder. I make achieving my goal – of finding any solution, let alone a solution that works for both of us – much more difficult. _I create the very resistance I'm trying to avoid._ I attract attention and push-back, instead of attention and engagement.

So BrainFishing is the art of attracting the right kind of attention. It's about consciously avoiding confrontation, while proactively – and intentionally – triggering the curious and intrigued response.

So, how do we do this?

## Brain Structure

First, a short lesson in brain structure. And one more Big Metaphor. Since we're talking about fishing for brains and not real fish, understanding how the human brain works is critical. We'll leave the important topic of how an actual fish brain works to the, uh, fish-ologists.

Very (very!) simply put, humans all come equipped with two different brains. What we'll call the Red Brain comprises two parts - the reptilian brain (the basal ganglia) and the paleo-mammalian brain (the limbic system, including the amygdala). These two parts of the Red Brain evolved first, and can be seen currently in creatures such as frogs and crocodiles (reptiles), and rabbits and tigers (mammals). These parts of our brain are specialized at keeping us alive in one of two ways: hunting, fighting, and killing; or running, hiding, and avoiding being killed. And boy is the Red Brain ever good at this!

The other brain we all have we can call the Blue Brain. This is the pre-frontal cortex, the so-called "higher brain", the rational, self-aware, thinking brain. The size of our Blue Brain is what makes us human, conscious, and different than almost all other species.

Back to the Red Brain and what it does for us. The Red Brain is always on, always working. Day and night, it is scanning the environment for one of two things – treats or threats. When the Red Brain sees a treat, it goes after it. When the Red Brain sees a threat, it goes into emergency mode, what is known as "fight or flight[1]". It doesn't matter what threat triggers the Red Brain because the result is almost always the same – an immediate, unconscious reaction of fight or flight. Red Brain characteristics include:

- The Red Brain handles all unconscious processes – breathing, heart rate, first impressions of people, and all automatic or habitual actions. Have you ever gotten in your car preoccupied by something and driven home, but can't actually remember doing the driving – and yet, you arrived safely? Thank you, Red Brain!

- The Red Brain can process vast amounts of information in parallel, assessing input from all of your senses virtually simultaneously (at Comic-Con, this is referred to as "Spidey-sense").

1  Some cite a third reaction, called "freeze", which is neither fight nor flight. Unfortunately, when the brain thaws, it defaults back to either fight or flight.

- The Red Brain operates below the level of conscious thought, and it can react to the environment about five times faster than your Blue Brain.

Sounds pretty good, right? There is a problem, though – it uses all that capability and capacity for only one goal, which is to keep you safe and alive. And it does this by signalling "fight" or "flight" as quickly as possible. But there is a lot more to being effective than just surviving.

Over to the Blue Brain, and how it helps us not just survive, but thrive. The Blue Brain, when it is engaged and working, provides things like this:

- The Blue Brain is capable of sustained focus on a problem or issue, and is very good at finding creative ways to solve almost any kind of problem or issue.

- The Blue Brain is highly analytical, able to deal with complex information and complicated situations – but it works slowly, and can work on only one issue or problem at a time.

- The Blue Brain requires enormous resources from the body – the brain as a whole uses about 20% of the body's resources, and the Blue Brain uses the lion's share of this. (The full brain of a gorilla, for example, only uses 8% of their bodies' resources – they have much smaller Blue Brains.)

Basically, it is the Blue Brain that allows us to be conscious, rational, and intelligent problem-solvers. The Red Brain simply helps keep us alive and safe.[2]

Both of these functions are critically important. But there is an even bigger problem: when we are faced with a "problem" or "issue", one that

---

2   For a much more detailed and intelligent description of these two thinking systems or "brains", check out Chapter Three, or go directly to "*Thinking Fast and Slow*", by Daniel Kahneman. Kahneman calls them "System One" and "System Two", but they refer to broadly similar processes. Or try the Dr. Seuss classic "*One Brain, Two Brain, Red Brain, Blue Brain*".

triggers any feeling of threat or risk, our Red Brain kicks in first (roughly four to five times faster than the Blue Brain) and takes us instantly into a fight or flight response, right from the start.

When the Red Brain takes over in that fight or flight response, this is what happens:

* Our body starts pumping adrenaline. This kicks up our heart rate, numbs sensations of pain, tunnel visions our sight onto the threat, and jumps us into action – either attack or retreat, fight or flight.

* More significantly, the blood flow to rest of our brain, i.e. the Blue Brain, is severely restricted, if not actually turned off, because of the enormous resources it uses. In other words, our Blue Brain, our rational brain, is disabled even before it gets a chance to assess or understand the problem or issue in any depth! After all, if there is indeed a threat, the muscles need all the blood they can get to successfully run or rumble.

Reflect on this. Think of a time where you had to react quickly and make an urgent decision, and later thought to yourself, "How could I have been so stupid?!" Know this – it wasn't you (i.e. your Blue Brain); it was your Red Brain driving that bus.

Regardless, the most important outcome of a Red Brain takeover is this – *We stop thinking. Period.*[3]

Back on the savannah when we were physically in danger (which was, like, most of the time), our Red Brain kept us alive and did a great job. But the Red Brain is not very sophisticated. It knows a threat when it sees one, but it can't tell the difference between the threat of being attacked by a predator and the threat posed by an angry customer or boss. It reacts exactly the same way.

---

3   Numerous books and research papers have identified this under the heading of the "Amygdala Highjack". Google it. Or go to Chapter Three for more details.

## Pick a Brain, Any Brain

So, when our Red Brain is triggered, we go into either hunting (fight) or prey (flight) mode. But the reverse is also true – when we voluntarily choose to solve any given problem by hunting (i.e. telling and arguing), we are also triggering our Red Brain into action. When we spend our time declaring, demanding or ordering other people around, our Red Brain, and likely their Red Brain, is taking over. We both argue, defend, and resist. Or we ignore, hide, and avoid. And all of this behaviour means the issue or problem is not solved or resolved between the parties – it is either won or lost, or it stays completely unresolved. We are simply acting out a modern version of fight or flight.

Even worse, hunting – engaging our Red Brain with the other party's Red Brain – can threaten or damage the relationship. When operating in our Red Brain, we always see the other person as a threat to be addressed, not a partner to work with.

On the other hand, when the Blue Brain is in charge, we become curious, interested, and engaged. We naturally start asking questions instead of telling. And the reverse of this is also true – when we choose to solve a problem the BrainFishing way by asking questions instead of telling, we automatically engage the Blue Brain, both ours and theirs. It works in both directions. Leading with our Blue Brains also creates connections, partnerships, and strengthens our relationships.

To be clear – hunting does work sometimes. The deer is shot. The village has a feast. Everyone celebrates! It can, on the surface, succeed.

Consider this, however: While hunting can get you what you want at times, it does so in spite of, or at the expense of, the other person (think of the deer's experience of the feast for a minute). It is a short-term, win-lose strategy.

## BrainFishing: A Tale of Two Shifts – or "One Good Shift Begets Another"

The move from hunting to BrainFishing actually entails two shifts. And they are directly connected.

The First Shift occurs within our own Blue Brain when we make the conscious choice to stop telling, telling, telling, and intentionally start asking, asking, asking.

The First Shift, the foundational shift to BrainFishing is this – make the conscious choice to ask questions. Regularly. Yep, that's it. That simple. And just remember, "simple" is not the same thing as "easy". But simple is good.

And as you may have figured out – since your Blue Brain is fully engaged at the moment, right? – the First Shift is what actually creates the Second Shift. This Second Shift occurs in the brain of the other person, the person you are communicating with when you ask them a question. They shift from working out of their Red Brain, to engaging with you from their Blue Brain. They start working *with* you instead of *against* you. They become curious, they participate in creating sustainable win-win solutions to problems, and they help to establish a relationship based on consideration and respect. A good question is more than an invitation to think – it's an invitation to engage and collaborate.

So the First Shift – a conscious choice to ask good, relevant questions – generates the Second Shift, the move to deep and engaged problem solving. The Blue Brains take over, helping the two of you actually communicate and start to build a relationship of trust and respect.

In other words, one good shift begets another.

So BrainFishing is actually about Blue BrainFishing, it's about engaging and attracting the best part of each other, about two Blue Brains actually working to solve problems. It is about engaging the most creative part of each other's brains; it is about building effective working relationships; it is about singing the Red Brains softly to sleep so our Blue Brains can actually come out and play.

Remember, play can be vigorous, demanding, even rough and tumble at times. But when you are fishing for Blue Brains and you catch them, you are engaging the very best in everyone around the table. Blue Brains working together get faster and better outcomes than fighting with our Red Brains ever can. And BrainFishing is the specific way we attract, lure, and engage other people's Blue Brains. We make the First Shift. The First Shift in us causes the Second Shift in the other person. The result is two Blue Brains collaborating to solve problems.

## The Shift to Fishing: Why Pick up that Rod?

Is this really going to make that much of a difference? The answer is an emphatic *yes*. Perhaps a table will help.

Here are some characteristics of telling, and what it changes into when we consciously shift to questioning. The First Shift causes some fundamental changes in our behaviour, which looks something like this:

### TABLE 1: The First Shift

| TELLING causes us to: | QUESTIONING helps us to: |
| --- | --- |
| Assert | Listen |
| Avoid | Engage |
| Argue | Inquire |
| Prove | Understand |
| Convince | Learn |
| Debate | Converse |
| Win | Win-Win |
| Be right | Be smarter |

| TELLING causes us to: | QUESTIONING helps us to: |
| --- | --- |
| Force the issue | Seek a solution |
| Fight | Collaborate |
| Narrow | Expand |
| Shut down | Open up |
| Minimize | Optimize |
| Denigrate | Respect |
| Attack | Embrace |
| Reject | Invite |

The common thread you might see above is this: telling triggers the Red Brain, and the Red Brain does what it is good at – attack or defend, fight or give in (and get out). Questioning engages, hooks, coaxes out the Blue Brain – and together, our Blue Brains are pretty darn good at solving problems, resolving issues, and even managing conflict.

There is a famous saying: "People are brilliant problem-solvers – *when they are in a problem solving frame of mind.*"[4] The real problem is that much of the time we are not in a problem solving frame of mind.

Much of the time, when the Red Brain is running the show, we spend all of our time trying to win, to be right, to feel respected, to be accepted, to be appreciated, to be heard. In Red Brain, we may also be trying to punish the other person, to prove they're wrong, to teach them a lesson. When we are fighting for recognition and acceptance, or fighting to teach someone a lesson, it's just that – a fight. And an unwinnable fight, in the longer term, at that. Say hello to Red Brain.

4   Okay, we said this, so it's not so famous. Yet.

Ask yourself this: When I feel attacked, minimized, rejected, shut down – how creative am I at solving a problem, any problem? How outside the box is my thinking? Even if I manage to "win" and succeed at getting my way through arguing, pushing, hounding, guilting, maybe even bullying, the other party is generally nowhere near as happy as I am. If they feel they've lost, they may well be secretly hoping I fail rather than succeed. And if they are actually hoping I will fail because of how I treated them, they may well look for opportunities to help that along. They may well start working against my interests or my success – and who needs that?

So, this comes down to a choice. Do I choose to get my way with great effort and leave the other person yearning to see me fail? Yearning to say "I told you so?" Or do I choose an approach where the other party is completely invested, just like me, in the solution working, and working well?

Choose wisely, Grasshopper.

## The Obviosity of it All

So, we need to break this habit of tell, tell, and tell. Great. This may start to seem a bit too obvious, too simplistic to actually make much of a difference. But if it's really so obvious and simple, why have so many people not figured it out? Why is "telling" still so popular?

The reason is deep, and layered, and is probably just baked into our nature as human beings. So, to that end, we'll start by letting everyone off the hook for this. When you get into arguments, fights, stalemates – it's not your fault. And it's not the other person's fault either.

The fault, if there is fault here, is not in our intentions, but in our reactions.

In other words, our constant falling into hunting/prey processes, into judgment and Red Brain behaviour, is not because we choose it – it is often thrust upon us. We automatically and unconsciously make the choice to protect ourselves, so the real culprit is that feeling of being threatened. And we feel this regularly, many times each and every day, in many different situations, particularly when we are under stress[5].

Our Red Brain has one job, as we said – to protect us, and keep us alive. It is highly sensitive to threats of any kind – physical threats, disrespect, threats to status, self-worth, ego, etc. It sees threats miles before they get close, and it reacts long before your Blue Brain can step in to handle the situation more effectively. The sequence often goes like this:

▶ I sense or believe you are angry with me – based on your tone, attitude, etc.

▶ Before I can stop and think it through my Red Brain reacts, getting defensive and pushing back.

▶ You, who were simply having a bad day for other reasons, feel the defensive attitude and the push-back, see this as a threat, and shove back the other direction.

▶ I feel the shove back, which confirms that you are indeed angry with me and attacking me and I react to protect myself by attacking back.

▶ You clearly feel the attack back from me, have had enough and retreat the other way – judging me to be insensitive and uncaring, vowing to show me the same lack of courtesy the next time around.

▶ I now feel vindicated and safe – I seem to have won! – until the next time, when I get an attack from you (totally out of the blue – or Red, in this case) that triggers the whole cycle again.

And both of us, and our Red Brains, feel that we were right, the other was wrong, and we carry this judgment into the next encounter – which unfolds the same way, only stronger. We both keep trying to gain the point, prove we are right, to *win*. And when we win, we feel justified for a short period of time. We rarely stop to consider what was actually won in the end.

5   In many cases, we are also unconscious of how threatened we feel – we just label it as "stress" or "a bad day". And then we spend our entire day in Red Brain, exhausted and demoralized.

Here's a milder version, characterized by best intentions and lots of telling:

- ▶ I get a great idea, a solution to a long-standing problem, and I rush to *tell* you.

- ▶ I start to *tell* you the solution (which, of course, is not perfect, no matter how good), and you listen and immediately see a few things this doesn't solve. You *tell* me what it *won't* fix.

- ▶ I argue it will fix a bunch of stuff, and keep *telling* you different parts of the solution.

- ▶ You interrupt and *point out* another situation it won't fix.

- ▶ I'm really annoyed now since you're not getting the message of how good this idea is, so I *challenge* you to put a better solution forward.

- ▶ You *tell* me an idea of your own, which I then happily challenge, *telling* you the many things your idea won't fix.

- ▶ You are now annoyed, and *tell* me my idea needs a lot of work.

- ▶ I'm now annoyed, and *tell* you your idea is terrible compared to mine.

- ▶ We both walk away annoyed, planning to avoid the other person going forward.

**Scoring Update: Red Brains: 2 Blue Brains: 0**

## ENOUGH! This (Parrot)Fish is Dead!

Enough about the problem. It is this core interaction, this First Shift to deliberately engaging others instead of pushing and directing others, that can improve 90% of your interactions. By making the First Shift, we cause the Second Shift in the other person, allowing us both to be more effective.

BrainFishing is about capturing their interest, inviting them to play, to think, to be creative. It's about carving the pegs to fit the holes, instead of pounding harder.

So let's get on with it and head out to the fishing hole. But before we can actually leave, we have to get ready, pack a cooler, and most importantly, make sure we understand the final ingredient in successfully making the First Shift so that it will lead to the Second Shift.

## First Shift, Second Shift – and Intention

The move from hunting to fishing, from hunting to the kind of fishing we're talking about – BrainFishing – has one final requirement: intention.

We have suggested that fishing is substantially different than hunting – and it can be. But fishing can also be about catching, gutting and eating the fish. And if that is the goal, then fishing is no different than hunting. It will still be about dominating or defeating the other party.

BrainFishing as a way to create dramatically different and better outcomes, on the other hand, has to have a different starting point, a different goal, a different *intention*. Think of this as a three step process.

### STEP #1 – Make the First Shift

The first step is consciously choosing to shift from telling to asking in many of our interactions.

When we make this First Shift, when we start asking, when we listen with patience, this shift in us creates the Second Shift in them.

### STEP #1
### The First Shift

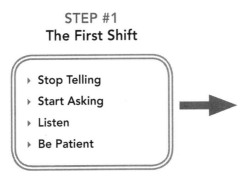

> ‣ **Stop Telling**
> ‣ **Start Asking**
> ‣ **Listen**
> ‣ **Be Patient**

### STEP #2 – They Engage and Make the Second Shift

A good question invites their Blue Brain to engage in the interaction. They make the Second Shift, and we both are in the land of problem solving. Our shift helps create their shift.

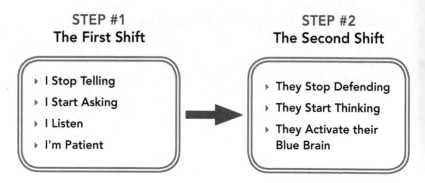

| STEP #1<br>**The First Shift** | STEP #2<br>**The Second Shift** |
| --- | --- |
| ▸ I Stop Telling<br>▸ I Start Asking<br>▸ I Listen<br>▸ I'm Patient | ▸ They Stop Defending<br>▸ They Start Thinking<br>▸ They Activate their Blue Brain |

What ultimately makes this work, however, rests with Step #3.

### Step #3 – Intention Determines Success

The stark difference between hunting and BrainFishing ultimately rests on intention. On what, deep down, you are trying to do or to accomplish.

Intention is a conscious choice. What is my goal in this interaction, this transaction, this negotiation, this relationship?

If you go into the interaction with a true "catch and release" mindset, with the intention that you will actively work toward a solution or agreement that listens to and respects the other person, that benefits *both parties*, then BrainFishing is the sport for you. BrainFishing will succeed short term and long term in almost every interaction or relationship you have.

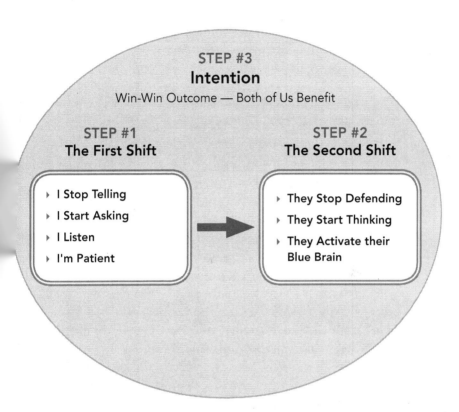

But if our intention is self-centred, if we are in it only to achieve *our* objectives, then we are hunting and not BrainFishing. If our intention is one-sided or self-serving, even if we think we are fishing, we are just a hunter in disguise. It may work once or twice, but *prey learn quickly*. You will simply be back to hunting – and back to being cold and alone in the woods.

## Intention: Collaboration or Manipulation?

It has been suggested to us that BrainFishing is just another form of manipulation – just more clever than most. As much as we hate begging, in this case we strongly beg to differ. Collaboration and manipulation are simply two sides of the same coin. When we flip that coin, what determines which side lands facing up comes down to this – our intention.

Influencing others, helping them to see the problem differently, changing their perspective – these goals in and of themselves are neither good nor bad, honest nor dishonest. But they can become either, based on our intention in every case. For example, if my intention is to get what I want at all costs, if my goal is to meet my own needs and I'm simply using you to achieve that – most of us see that as manipulative and dishonest. But if my intention is to get what I need *and* help you to get what you need at the same time, if my goal is a win-win solution, then my behaviour will be seen as collaborative and honest. In both cases, I'm trying to get what I need, but only in the win-win case will I be seen as honourable, fair – and most importantly, trustworthy. Intention makes all the difference.

So ask yourself regularly – what is my intention? Is it just about me, or do I truly want a solution that works for both of us? Am I simply manipulating the conversation to get what I want or am I authentically working to create a genuine win-win outcome? With the right intention, BrainFishing can be ridiculously easy to learn and get good at. It will ultimately make us more effective problem-solvers and lead to more productive and satisfying relationships.

## Heading to the Fishing Hole

So here's the test to see if this Practice Guide will work for you: If the idea of being able to create real connection and engagement in every interaction appeals to you, read on! But if you're a happy, successful hunter who enjoys having victims rather than partners – thanks for stopping by. Just think of us when another hunter gets the drop on you, and ask yourself if it's time for a change.

For those still on the ride with us, the next chapter is all about the "*How*" – how to make the First Shift happen, when and how to apply it, and what language best leads us to true BrainFishing rather than hunting.

So – truck warmed up, intentions clear, dry clothing packed, and a new sign now hanging on the door....

Here we go!

Chapter Two

# A Practice Guide to Questioning Skills

Ahhh! Still here. Excellent!

So let's get down to it. This is a Practice Guide, so let's get to the practice part.

The First Shift, as we discussed, is simple. Stop telling. Ask questions. Stop hunting. Start BrainFishing. This, of course, sounds easy when you say it quickly – Sure! Just ask questions! No problem!!!

In reality, this First Shift, the shift in *our* behaviour, is one that requires us to change a habit. Telling is nothing more than a habit – but a deeply ingrained one – taught to us from a very, very young age.

> **SCENE:** Mary is in grade one and the teacher helpfully asks, "Mary, what is one plus one?" Mary, having read this Practice Guide, helpfully asks back, "Um, why do you need to know that, Mr. Bassman?"
> **CUT TO:** Mary, in detention, writing on the blackboard "I will answer the teacher's question..." 500 times...Message received...
> *FADE TO BLACK*

Yet telling, like many habits, can be replaced by better, more effective habits. To learn how to question, and question well, we'll work through the following:

### Lesson 1: *Basic BrainFishing Equipment*

Before actually fishing, it would be good to understand a bit about the "equipment". In this case, the equipment is an understanding of the art and science of the question. We'll spend some time with the basics of questioning.

### Lesson 2: *Baiting the Hook, Casting and Reeling*

Once we understand the basics about questioning (and it ain't rocket science), it's important to think about the "bait" – what do we ask about that will engage Blue Brains, attract them, make them think? What can we put in front of them that will attract them and engage them? What is the target, the focus of our questions? And finally, what will entice Blue Brains to engage in a good problem-solving conversation?

### Lesson 3: *Filling The Tackle Box*

Once we are comfortable with the basics of questioning, and once we start baiting, casting and reeling, what equipment is there for more advanced BrainFishing? We'll show you the many different questions, the many lures, hooks, and flies that you have available to you to accomplish specific goals and to address different kinds of problems. In other words, when faced with different kinds of people and different situations, you can use different approaches with different tools in order to effectively attract Blue Brains.

### *Exercises and Fish Stories*

Throughout all of the lessons, we'll give you exercises to practice your own personal fishing skills, and tell you some stories from our experience and the experience of other effective questioners. All of them true. None of them, well, fishy.

Let's go!

**Basic BrainFishing Equipment**

**PART 1: Understanding Questions**

The First Shift, from hunting to fishing, starts as simply as this: Ask questions. Stop telling. Ask questions.

So, let us make this fancy and suitable for framing:

> ## Ask Questions.
> ## Stop Telling.
> ## Ask Questions.

If it were this easy, however, we'd all be doing it and you wouldn't need this book (even though our book is cheap enough for you to buy five, even 10 copies for friends). So let's go deeper into this idea, and what this First Shift really means.

For starters, anyone can ask a question, but many times it doesn't actually shift anything. For example:

Father sitting in the dark as the teenager sneaks into the house, four hours past curfew:

> TEENAGER: Oh! You scared me, Dad.
>
> DAD: I scared you!? *Don't you think I'm scared, sitting here for hours not knowing if you're dead or alive? Do you know how upset your mother is!?*

Boss to an employee who is late delivering a report:

> EMPLOYEE: Here is the report, sorry it's late.
>
> BOSS: Sorry!? *Do you know what this delay has done to my reputation with the Director!?*

You will note, in both cases, questions were asked. But is this really fishing? Or just telling in disguise?

Remember, the purpose of questions, the purpose of the First Shift, the shift from hunting to fishing, is clear – it is to:

1. attract and engage the other person's Blue Brain without triggering their Red Brain, and

2. gather good information that will help the Blue Brains in the room effectively solve the problem.

In both examples above, while the dad and the boss have both, technically, asked questions, those questions are not really questions at all – they are judgments disguised as questions. They are conclusions, arguments, attacks, and accusations disguised as questions. No shift at all.

So, the First Shift is the shift to questions – real questions. And to understand what makes a question a "real" question, to become good at the art of questioning, we have to see that questions must, at their base, be judgment-free.

## This is a Judgment-Free Zone

While telling triggers that opposing reaction, the content of *what* we choose to tell people often makes it even worse. We all have a few "default settings" – entrenched biases that instantly and forcefully trigger the Red Brain, both in us and in the person we are telling.

You may be familiar with this quote: "Judge not, lest you be judged." Yes, we're going to go all biblical for a moment. And while the quote is indeed biblical, it serves as a key principal in most other great religions (and philosophies) in the world.

It turns out that one thing that we are all exceptionally good at, from a young age, is this: judging other people. We love to judge others. We gravitate to seeing others as wrong, as foolish, as making bad choices. We love to see ourselves as right, as smart, as always making good choices. After all, this feels good. We like to feel solid, safe, and wise. And one of the best ways to feel solid, safe and wise is to see others as foolish, making bad choices and suffering the consequences. We (well, the Germans, at least) even have a word for it – *Schadenfreude* – the pleasure derived from another person's misfortune.

And what is the quickest way to feel solid, safe and wise? By telling others *they* are wrong, and then showing them why *we* are right. We judge them, plain and simple. And we do it a lot. Telling (and hunting), you'll note, is almost always a sign of judgment. I'm right – *and you're not*.

Whether we do this consciously (sometimes) or unconsciously (much more common), we judge others as a way of protecting ourselves. Feeling "right" puts us in a defensible, superior position. It signals to our Red Brain that we're on top, making us feel strong and safe. But this power-ful-feeling Red Brain position severely limits us in successfully solving real, tangible problems and, perhaps more importantly, from building long-term, productive, sustainable relationships. A key part of the First Shift, therefore, is shifting away from judgment.

Ask yourself this: How does it make you feel when *you* are being judged? Not so warm and fuzzy. In fact, the biggest problem with judging others is this: while *we* feel strong and safe, we make *them* feel threat-ened, triggering their Red Brain into action. They attack and judge us in return, now making us feel threatened, triggering us into our Red Brain. And we both head into the Red Brain boxing ring for a bruising session of "Who is Right? Who is Wrong?" Who wins, in the end, usually doesn't matter. The only guarantee is that everyone leaves feeling emotionally battered and bruised.

From the examples above, it should be clear that when our intent is to judge, when we go all judgmental on someone else, even questions won't save us. The judgment shines through.

So, a key part of Lesson 1 about the basics of questioning, and of mak-ing the First Shift, is this:

## We must default to Curiosity, not Judgment.

So, to recap. Judgment is aggressive, judgment triggers the Red Brain directly into fight or flight mode and sends the Blue Brain into hiding.

The First Shift is intended to do the opposite. It is intended to calm the Red Brain and attract the Blue Brain. And Blue Brains require an environment where it's safe to come out and play, to come closer, to be interested enough to take up the bait. Blue Brains need to be enticed, not threatened.

To attract Blue Brains, we must exploit two built-in features that all Blue Brains have when they are engaged: 1) they are incredibly curious, and 2) they need to be listened to and heard. To leverage this toward effective engagement, we must become just as curious as they are and very interested in listening to and hearing what they have to say. We must ask questions, yes, and ask every question with genuine curiosity, with a real desire to hear the answer – not judge it.

For greater clarity, this is not a metaphysical issue. You do not have to reach an extreme state of Zen, you do not have to empty yourself of all ego, you do not have to become One with the other Blue Brain – you simply have to be curious about the answer. Genuinely curious and willing to listen. Try a simple way to practice this: On your notepad for your next meeting, write the following block letters in the upper right corner: **AQ-SUL.** Every few minutes, let your eyes wander over to those letters as a clear reminder. These letters stand for:

## Ask a Question – Shut Up and Listen.

And every time you read this, check on your behaviour. Are you telling, or are you listening? And what can you do to make sure you are listening while someone else talks? AQ, then SUL.

AQ is the easy part. It's the SUL that's hard. Think of it this way: After you ask a question and as they are talking, try to actually learn something from what they are saying:

- *Why does this make sense to them? ...Ah! That's why!*
- *What are they trying to accomplish? ...Okay, that's clear now!*

* *What are they concerned about? ...Really? That's their concern? Didn't expect that!*

If you can start to learn from the answers to these questions as they are talking, then you are truly listening and not judging. And if their answers aren't clear, then actually ask those questions – out loud. One of the greatest values of good questions and serious listening is that it helps the other party clarify their own thinking. When an individual discovers or develops a solution for themselves it is far more powerful than being told or given the exact same solution.

## PART 2: Asking the Right Type of Question

The second step in understanding the art of questioning is using the right type of question. It turns out that the broad type of question you ask makes a huge difference. Later, in the tackle box section, we'll give you a bunch of different subtypes of questions that can help you land big whopping Blue Brains, once you have engaged them. Staying with the basics for now, however, we want to encourage those Blue Brains to come out and play – to get them thinking, get them talking, and get them deeply engaged. Remember, BrainFishing is about attracting and engaging the thinking part of the brain, the Blue Brain, by calming the Red Brain.

To do that, the broad type of question you ask must be open questions, not closed.[1]

We know what you're thinking – *Wow, Captain Obvious, everyone knows this!* Yes, most of us do know the difference between open and closed questions. Say it with us: "Closed questions are the 'Yes/No' questions. Open questions are the five W's and H – Who What When Where Why[2] and How". Most of us know this. The problem is that we just don't make the shift into actually using open questions.

---

1   In the tackle box section, we'll give you specific uses for closed questions, too. But first, you must master the open question.
2   Note that for many people, "why" is just as problematic as closed questions are. Why? Oops, we mean, "the reason?" We don't know, we just find that starting most questions with "what", or "how" gets us big fat Blue Brain engagement, whereas "why" seems to call the demon Red Brain from hiding.

So, open questions. Any question that starts with one of the 5 W's or H (*and* is genuinely curious!) has a very good chance of achieving two things:

- First, it will engage the other Blue Brain and start them thinking.
- Second, it will push our own Blue Brain toward curiosity rather than judgment.

### Table 1: **Closed Questions**

**Take a look at these simple, common questions:**

| |
|---|
| *Didn't you finish that report yet?* |
| *Were you, or were you not, aware of our deadline for this?* |
| *Are you saying you're happy with these results?* |
| *Haven't you spoken to the client about this yet?* |
| *Do you actually know how to do this?* |
| *Haven't you finished your homework yet?* |

As you read these, what do these questions make you feel like or think about? How effectively do they open you up? Calm you down? Make you want to roll up your sleeves and work with the person asking them?

We didn't think so.

Closed questions like these feel like accusations, like finger-pointing, like – well, like judgments. They tend to make us want to defend, to debate, to argue, and to show the questioner that they are wrong. Red Brain heaven!

Now look at the same questions on the left, but transformed into open questions on the right. What do the questions on the right side, in contrast, tend to make you feel like and think about?

## Table 2: Closed Questions to Open Questions

| Closed Questions: | Open Questions: |
| --- | --- |
| *Didn't you finish that report yet?* | *How far along is the report?* |
| *Were you, or were you not, aware of our deadline for this?* | *What was the deadline you were working toward?* |
| *Are you saying you're happy with these results?* | *How do you feel about these results?* |
| *Haven't you spoken to the client about this yet?* | *When you spoke to the client, what was their response?* |
| *Do you actually know how to do this?* | *How much experience have you had with this?* |
| *Haven't you finished your homework yet?* | *How much homework do you have left to do?* |

If you react like most, the questions on the left, even if asked in an "innocent" way, carry an edge to them, a sense of risk, of accusation even. In contrast, the questions on the right feel a bit safer – a bit more, well, *open!*

There is a reason for this. Closed questions, no matter how nicely they are asked, almost always have a *right* and a *wrong* answer – there is a judgment embedded in the question itself. They often feel like a trick question, sometimes described as a "lawyer question"[3] – or worse, a police interrogation.

Take the last question on the left side in Table 2. When a parent asks their child the question "Haven't you finished your homework yet?", the

---

3    And to be fully fair to lawyers, these are appropriate questions in the courtroom, since the goal at trial is *not* to problem solve, but to win the case, to show their client to be right, to help the judge, well, *judge* the other party. They are effective for that goal – but not for our goal of problem solving.

child *knows* the right answer to that question the instant it is asked. And they will likely try and find a way to give their parent the right answer. Why? The right (and by extension wrong) answer was plain to see, and it evoked a strong Red Brain reaction. When a parent asks the question on the right side, however, the child would actually have to think, to engage, and to give more information and a deeper explanation.[4] And they'd have a chance to actually talk about the situation.

## SUMMARY

> **LESSON 1**

### Basic BrainFishing Equipment

So, Lesson 1 is simple:

- ask questions
- stop telling
- ask open questions
- lose the judgments
- be genuinely curious

This, in a nutshell, is the First Shift, the shift away from hunting and the start of true BrainFishing.

> **EXERCISE #1[5]**

### Curiosity and Open Questions

A man stops a woman on a street in New York City, and asks, "How do I get to Carnegie Hall?" The woman replies, "Practice, practice, practice."

---

4   As we said, questions that start with either "what" or "how" seem to have the highest potential to attract Blue Brains of all the open questions.

5   We have captured every exercise in the BrainFishing Worksheets section at the back, where you will find ample space to actually do the exercises, write stuff down, and practice, practice, practice!

An old joke, yes. A true statement? Also yes. If you want to make that First Shift, if you want the benefits of engaged, authentic problem solving with other people, well, you need to practice. So, just a few simple exercises to help you play with Lesson 1:

## Judgment and Curiosity Exercise

- **Fun with Judgment:** The next time you are talking to someone about anything, and we mean anything, try this – tell them at least twice that they are wrong. Dead wrong. Flat out wrong. Period. And watch their Red Brain leap in to argue, defend, get angry, etc. (Tip: don't do this on date night…).

- **Fun with Curiosity:** Then, suddenly shift to being genuinely curious. Ask questions to understand, to clarify. Be genuinely interested. Thank them for what you just learned – and then ask another question to learn more. Watch their Blue Brain slowly emerge, watch them calm down, relax, and give you lots and lots of information (and, if it's date night, enthusiastic attention…).

## Open and Closed Question Exercise

- **Fun with Closed Questions:** The next time you talk to your teenager or partner, ask them a string of deliberately closed questions. "Did you… Aren't you… Couldn't you have… Don't you agree that…?" Watch carefully what happens, and as the closed questions continue, watch for the other person starting to get defensive, annoyed, upset – classic Red Brain symptoms (Tip: Don't let this go on too long…).

- **Fun with Open Questions:** After their Red Brain is fully apparent, switch to open questions: "What do you think about…? Tell me more about… How might we…? What other ideas do you have about…?" See how long it takes for their Blue Brain to come out and play, how quickly they calm down, start thinking again, relax, and engage.

Congratulations! You've just dipped your hook in the fishin' pond, and purposefully attracted your first Blue Brain!

## FISH STORIES — "Strike a Blow for Lunch Breaks!"

A union that represented social services workers went on strike after their employer demanded that their paid lunch be given up, which the union refused. The harder management demanded that the paid lunch be given up, the harder the union rejected the suggestion. Finally, an 84 day strike took place. Eventually, the government ordered them back to work, ending with the award of a status quo contract. The paid lunch stayed.

Two years later, they were back at the bargaining table. This time, anticipating the same issue and another strike, both parties requested a mediator. First issue up? The paid lunch.

Each party started to replay the last round. Management proposed the paid lunch be given up, and the union, predictably, rejected it. This time, however, the mediator asked one question of the union: "What is the reason you are so strongly opposed to giving up the paid lunch?" The room settled down. The union explained, forcefully, that many times, clients came into the office over the lunch break and the workers always served them, many times missing their lunch break. It was only fair that it was paid, since they often worked right through it. The mediator turned to management, and asked one more question: "What's the reason you're so adamant that the paid lunch be given up?" They also settled down, and explained clearly that the funding for it had been cut by the government two years ago, and that money was being taken directly from client services to pay for it.

The mediator then asked one more question of both parties: "What could you do to make sure employees are always paid for the work they do, even if it takes place during lunch?"[6] After a pause, management proposed that employees have the right to "bank" any time they work during lunch, and take it off when they didn't have clients. The lunch itself would be unpaid, but all work done during lunch would be paid with an equal amount of time off after the appointment. The union agreed.

*BrainFishing Analysis: Imagine, an 84 day strike because too much telling led directly to an impasse, to a strike that benefited no one, all for the want of three simple, and open, questions? Once it was safe to actually think, to talk, and to be heard, the parties solved the problem in about two hours.*

### FISH STORIES — "Make My Year!"

An account manager who sold auto parts to companies with large fleets of vehicles was referred to the warehouse manager of a large fleet-servicing shop, where mechanics serviced hundreds of small trucks and vans for deliveries. The referral came with a warning: the warehouse manager liked to eat salespeople for lunch!

The account manager started to prepare detailed slides, stories and brochures to "wow" the warehouse manager with how attentive he was as an account manager, how great his company was, how they carried a full range of quality products and offered the highest quality service – basically, a "Tell-Fest"! After attending a BrainFishing event, he scrapped the slides and came up with a short list of four open questions instead:

---

6   See Chapter Two in the tackle box for a description of this specific kind of question. It's a good example of an open question, but it's also a Problem Solving question, a type that is very useful to have at your disposal.

1. How are you trying to grow your business?
2. What is the most important thing a product supplier can do to make you successful?
3. What are the greatest risks you face?
4. How can I best support you?

The warehouse manager started talking and could barely be stopped. What was supposed to be a 30-minute introductory meeting turned into a 90-minute problem solving session. The account manager won the business, and within three months the fleet shop was his largest account. And yes, it made his year, with the result being a new and growing business relationship and a very healthy year-end bonus. All from taking up a new hobby – BrainFishing...

**BrainFishing Analysis:** *Not only were these questions more effective in the meeting, but think about how much time is wasted on creating long, boring PowerPoint presentations that clients sleep through. The BrainFishing approach is not only more effective, but often far more efficient as well.*

### ▶ LESSON 2

**Baiting the Hook, Casting, and Reeling**

**PART 1: Baiting the Hook**

So, using open questions and practicing genuine curiosity are the basic equipment for BrainFishing. That's a good start. But before you cast some of those questions into the water, you need to have the right bait.

In other words, is just flinging any old question onto the table enough?

As we saw, the short answer is "No!" Not all questions work to attract and engage Blue Brains. Closed questions and judgmentality scare the fish away, big time.

So beyond understanding open and closed questions, we have to ask – "What is it in the content of the question itself that will best draw the attention of the Blue Brain? What will attract it, entice it to open up, to come out and play?"

The answer is the same when fishing for actual fish – the right bait, or an attractive lure. Bait in the real fishing world is food, tasty tidbits that are irresistible. Lures are bits of colour or fluffy stuff that simply resemble tasty tidbits and are also irresistible. So what is irresistible to Blue Brains?

## It's All About Me – ME

It is said that everyone's favourite radio station is WIIFM – "What's In It For Me?" In other words, the topic that is most attractive to each individual person is *themselves* – what *they* want, what *they* need, are concerned about, are hoping for. What can *they* get, gain, or achieve? Some of this is pure self-interest – what they can gain, achieve or get for themselves, personally. But well beyond that, WIIFM also represents a wide range of things that people see as important, valuable and meaningful, often well beyond their own personal gain.

To be clear, the strongest, most attractive bait for each and every one of us is this: what I see as my wants, my needs, my fears, my concerns and my hopes.

- Ask me about what I want – I love talking about that!

- Ask me what I need – I'll happily tell you that.

- Ask me what I'm afraid of or concerned about – you'll get an earful.

- Ask me about my hopes, dreams, desires, what is important to me – how much time do you have?!

So when we go BrainFishing, when we need to attract and engage Blue Brains, the best bait and lures in the world are topics and ideas that the other person will connect with, will gravitate to, have a strong opinion on. These sorts of topics tap into what they are dying to tell you about: their wants, their needs, their fears or concerns, their hopes and dreams. These turn out to be Blue Brain crack.

We generically call these topics, and more specifically what that person wants or needs, "interests". Ask someone about their interests, and – instant engagement! – they will talk as long as you will listen. You've just engaged with a Blue Brain!

So let's unpack this idea of bait. Let's open the can of worms and pour it on the table.

## The Three Kinds of Bait

There are three different kinds of bait, three different types of interests[7] that people are always trying to get met. The better we understand these three types of bait or interests, the more effectively we will engage each other to solve problems rather than fight. We'll take them one at a time.

## The Obvious Bait – The Result

The most obvious interest we all have is an interest in the result, the outcome, the actual solution that is implemented in any given situation. We want the solution we have always dreamed of, the outcome that suits us best, the answer we desire. The result is the most tangible interest we have; it's the one we talk the most about because it's the most obvious and easy to identify, to see, to ask for, or to fight about. Results look like this:

- An employee wants a particular week off for vacation.
- A car buyer wants a lower price.

---

7   For an even deeper dive into these three types of interests, see Chapter 5: The Triangle of Satisfaction in "The Conflict Resolution Toolbox" by Gary T. Furlong, Wiley and Sons, 2005.

- A homeowner wants permission to build an addition on their home.

- A plaintiff wants all the money they sued the defendant for.

The list is long, but it will ultimately focus on the specific answer or outcome that is desired. Everyone in the world is keenly attuned to getting what they want, getting the answer or result that they think they need. So, the result is a particularly important type of interest that will immediately engage a Blue Brain in a discussion about what it wants, and why.

Go ahead and try this on your own. Ask anyone, in any situation, what they want and why it is important to them – you'll get the full answer, in depth, for as long as you care to listen. Just try and stop them! You will get more information than you thought possible. Their Blue Brain is now engaged, nibbling at the bait, and giving you lots of information along the way.

But even with how interested they now are to talk with you, there are two other types of bait that can be even more attractive to people than simply getting the result or outcome they want.

## The Quieter Bait – The Process

A less obvious type of bait for the Blue Brain is the "process" – the specific approach that is taken to achieve those results. Since most Blue Brains (and even most Red Brains) understand that no one gets the outcome they want all the time, the result can at times be a spotty or inconsistent motivator. Many of us realize, for example, that when we get our first job we are not going to be offered a million dollars in salary. There just aren't many of those jobs around. Sadly.

So, the next important interest we have is not about the result or outcome, but about the structure or framework, the *process* within which we arrive at any given result. And what we all insist on, even demand, is that the process, framework, or structure, answers to two fundamental human needs:

1. **Is the process clear?** First, we need to know what is going on, what is going to happen next if we're going to quiet our Red Brain and engage our Blue Brain. When we think we're about to be blindsided or surprised, we tend to unleash the Red Brain to "fix" the problem! (And when we feel stupid or embarrassed, this unleashes the Red Brain, too.)

2. **And most important: Is the process, the structure, or the framework seen as "fair"?** The process, structure or framework we work within sets the context and establishes meaning. It is this context and meaning that allows us to judge or assess the fairness of the result. We hate being treated unfairly more than just about anything else *(how many people have driven all the way back to the grocery store because the cashier accidentally scanned the can of tuna twice? It likely wasn't the 99 cents...).*

Clarity and fairness of the process are strong and deep interests; because of this, focusing on the process used to arrive at a solution is a powerful attractor for Blue Brains. For example, if you're an accountant who has been out of work for a few months, it's likely you would happily accept an accounting job offer that pays the average accounting salary of $80k per year. All is good. That is, until you find out a month into the job that every other accountant in this company is paid over $100k, even from when they were first hired! A great dissatisfaction sets in, the Red Brain starts working overtime, you feel tricked, undervalued, disrespected, and – wait a minute! Weren't you happy, even thrilled with the job and the pay just a day before? What changed?

What changed was your sense of fairness in the pay structure or salary framework in this company. While $80k in salary met all the result needs you had – it paid the mortgage, living expenses, even enough for a vacation – you suddenly became dissatisfied because the overall framework or context was now seen differently. You're paid less than other people for the same work. They took advantage of you. You feel as if you've been tricked. You want more. You either complain to your boss or the human resources department, or you start thinking about looking for another job that very day. When it no longer seemed fair, *the result by itself was not enough.* Fairness is a stronger motivator, a stronger bait, than most results.

Ask a Blue Brain about what they see as a fair process and framework and why they view it that way, and you will get a deep, long conversation about fairness and justice, about core values and deeper needs. It will immediately bring out their Blue Brain and will dramatically increase the chances of a satisfactory result.

### FISH STORIES — "Two Steps Forward..."

A large public hospital had been leasing the land and buildings for a local emergency ward in a remote part of the city. The lease was up, and the board of the hospital had to re-negotiate the lease rate. The landlord was a medium-sized religious organization, a church. Both the hospital and the church wanted the hospital to remain as the tenant – in fact, the church had built a large retirement community and care facility beside it. Having a hospital literally next door was a big selling feature for people to retire there.

They could not, however, agree on a lease rate. The church insisted that the market value for the cheapest rent in the area for any kind of commercial or industrial building was approximately $7.00 per square foot. The hospital argued that since this building was purpose-built for a hospital, the only real comparators were other hospitals, and hospitals paid an average of $2.50 per square foot. Neither side would move.

After a long impasse, one party suggested a process to break the logjam. They suggested that each party retain a certified real estate appraiser, specialized in commercial real estate, and obtain a valuation for a new lease on a per square foot basis. The parties would then take the two valuations, average the two numbers the appraisers identified, and that average would be the new price for rent.

The two parties quickly agreed. The two appraisals came out and the new rate, averaged, was $3.23 per square foot. When the church was asked how they felt about losing, i.e. having ended up with a number far below the rent they had proposed, the board chair said, "We wanted a fair rate for our property. When the board looked at the process and the two appraisals, they felt the final number was fair. We are satisfied."

**BrainFishing Analysis:** *People will tend to accept outcomes they don't like if and only if they see the process as fair.*

## The Strongest Bait – The Emotions

The third type of bait is in many cases the strongest, the most attractive, and the most powerful. Emotional interests, also called psychological interests, often overpower the more obvious result and process interests. Many a time people have rejected a good result because of an even stronger desire for feeling respected, being right, or even wanting revenge. It happens every day.

A good example of emotional interests running the show can be seen in all civil courts in North America. The average amount of money in dispute in North American court cases is approximately $65,000. That is the amount the plaintiff is suing the defendant for, asking the court to award them. But the cost of hiring a lawyer, filing a claim, gathering evidence, conducting discovery or depositions, preparing for the trial, and going through the trial itself can easily be close to $70,000 – per party! This means that in the typical case, the two parties are jointly spending close to $140,000 in order to find out if the plaintiff will be awarded the $65,000.

Even if the plaintiff wins the case – and assuming they actually win all $65,000 – the best they will end up with is $30,000 in their pocket. Here's the math:

- If they win the full $65k, they must then deduct the $70k in costs they paid their own lawyer, leaving them with a $5k loss. But don't worry, they will also be awarded about $35k toward their legal costs[8] from the defendant. $65k - $70k + $35k = $30k net).

- If they lose the case, however, they risk collecting nothing from the defendant, still paying $70,000 to their lawyer, and being forced to pay another $35,000 to the defendant's lawyer for *their* legal costs – for a total loss of $105,000 ($0k - $70k - $35k = -$105k).

How many of you would place a $105,000 bet in Las Vegas when you have only a 50/50 chance of winning back a total of $30,000, and a 50/50 chance of losing all $105,000? Not very many.

Yet thousands of people sue other people every day, in every legal jurisdiction in North America! The question is – why?

The answer is simple – *it isn't about the money*. When litigants are asked what it's about if not the money, the answers vary but often sound very much like one of these:

- *I won't let them get away with it!*
- *I'm right – and I'm going to show them I am!*
- *It may cost me $70,000 – but it will cost them that much too!*
- *I want my day in court!*
- *It's a matter of principle!*

What every statement above tells us is that it has nothing to do with

---

8   In most court cases, the losing party is ordered to pay about half of the winning party's legal fees. No surprise that most people would rather be the lawyer than the litigant!

the result – the results are going to be poor in almost every case. What is motivating these litigants is simple – it's how they *feel*, or how they *want to feel*. And how we feel translates into a range of emotional or psychological interests, such as:

- Wanting to be right
- Wanting to win
- Wanting revenge
- Wanting to teach the other person a "lesson"

Not all emotional/psychological interests are negative. Some others include:

- Wanting to be heard, and understood
- Wanting recognition, acknowledgement, or an apology
- Wanting validation
- Wanting closure
- Wanting respect

These emotional interests are powerful motivators to the Blue Brain, and can also act as either powerful instigators or powerful sedatives for the Red Brain.

Here's a fun exercise for you to try to test how powerful these motivators are. The next time a friend of yours says anything, anything at all, just tell them they are wrong. Dead wrong. Or even better, that they are wrong and foolish to even think that. Then go whole hog, and tell them how disappointed you are in them. Should you actually survive, note how quickly they get angry, withdrawn or vengeful. If you're interested in even more fun, try this with your significant other. It will take days to recover![9]

---

9   Please note: If you didn't catch the tongue-in-cheek nature of this suggestion and actually try this one with your significant other, you are hereby releasing the authors from any and all liability for any actions their Red Brain may decide to inflict upon you.

## FISH STORIES — "I Just Want You To Listen!"

Crisis hotlines exist in many cities in North America as a resource to people who are desperate, depressed, or at the end of their rope. They are based on one fundamental approach – listen to the caller. Just listen. Let them know they have been heard. That's it. They have learned that suggesting a result or a solution to people in crisis, or even suggesting ways (processes) to feel better simply doesn't work. In fact, they make it worse. Listening, letting someone know they are being heard, is one of the only ways to ease the crisis, to calm the desperation of the Red Brain when it is triggered. The deep interest that needs to be met is emotional, not results or process. And in these very difficult cases, the only approach that works is acknowledging that need, asking gentle but direct emotion-based questions and then listening. Really listening.

At some point the caller is ready to ask for help – and when they do, the hotline staff have referrals to professional people and processes to get them the help they need. But that only comes after the emotional interests are met.

*BrainFishing Analysis: We see this in our personal lives, as well. Have you ever had a spouse come home complaining of having a hard day, and you tried to fix it for them? Given them ideas and solutions to make it better? And how many times have they gotten angry and told you they "just want you to listen!" Quite simply, we were trying to meet the wrong need. We focused on the result, the solution, the fix, when they needed an emotional interest met.*

### PART 2: Casting

So now we have our bait – interests. And as we said, people spend all day, every day, trying to get their interests met. All three types. We are trying to earn money, to succeed, to get a good deal, to have decisions go our way. We also demand fair treatment, equal treatment, consistent treatment, and to know how and why decisions are made. Lastly, we want to feel respected, to be heard, to be acknowledged for who we are, what we have achieved, to be right, to be a winner. Anything that helps us get any of these interests met will attract our attention. That is powerful bait, an almost irresistible attraction.

The next question we need to answer is this: How do we get these interests in front of them? How do we cast this bait to attract their attention?

The answer brings us back full circle: we engage their interests with questions, questions that are focused directly into their interests.

This might ring a bell – hunting is about telling. BrainFishing is about asking questions. To engage and attract the thinking part of another person's brain, the First Shift is to ask questions. And those questions must attract the Blue Brain and calm the Red Brain. The only way to do that is to ask questions that engage the Blue Brain and their most important interests. Bait the hook with what they want, what they need, what they are concerned about or hoping for. In other words, we cast the bait into the water with good questions.

Here are a few good questions loaded up with different kinds of bait, ready for casting:

#### Table 3: Questions Baited with Different Types of Interests

**Questions Baited with Result Interests**

---

- *What are you looking for here? What would solve this problem?*
- *How would you see allocating the bonuses to the team?*
- *What price are you willing to offer on the house?*
- *What have we missed with this solution?*

## Questions Baited with Process Interests

---

- *How long do you see this taking? How could we speed that up?*
- *What was the reasoning behind this decision?*
- *Who else would have good information for the project?*
- *When and how often should we meet?*
- *What other information might be important to consider?*
- *What would you see as fair here?*

## Questions Baited with Emotional Interests

---

- *What would you see as a respectful way to address this?*
- *How could we take your experience on this file into account?*
- *What would tell you that your concerns have been heard?*
- *How do you feel about this approach?*
- *How comfortable with this solution are you?*

Put these kinds of questions in front of any Blue Brain, and they will get engaged in a big way. Each question causes that other brain to stop and think about the important interests these questions have flagged. Once we have engaged that Blue Brain into thinking deeply about their important interests, we need to keep them moving deeper and deeper into helping find solutions to the problem. We need to help pull them all the way toward a good outcome.

## PART 3: Reeling

But how do we land these fish? What will help reel them in, draw them forward, keep them willing to stay engaged? What will help us draw the Blue Brains all the way into deep, focused problem solving?

In fishing terms, it's easy to get the fish to nibble and bite, but something has to "set the hook", to engage them deeply enough to keep them on the line even when there is emotion and tension, even when tackling difficult issues and challenges that will send most people running for cover. We have to know how to keep those Blue Brains engaged.

The most important part of reeling in Blue Brains is simple. It's called "listening".

Yeah, yeah, we hear many of you saying, "Sure. I listen all the time. But most of what I hear just sounds stupid, so am I supposed to just keep listening to that junk?" (*But no judgment, right?*) The short answer is – *Yes!* If you want to keep their Blue Brain engaged, hooked, and working with you, you must listen – but not just any kind of listening. You must listen and you must *hear* them. Many of us think of listening as simply not talking, as shutting up while the other person yammers on about their misguided ideas while we come up with much better ones – or reasons why they're wrong – in our head. This is not listening – it's *arguing*, just not out loud. Most Blue Brains pick up on that pretty quickly.

To effectively keep them engaged, to actually have the other person want to stay engaged and working to solve the problem, you must reel in their Blue Brain with actual, effective, and demonstrable listening.

Listening – or what we often refer to as listening – can be described on three levels.

1. **Level One Listening – *Surface*.** This type of listening is basically when we are pretending to listen. Often referred to as "surface" listening, it happens when the other person is talking and we are on a mental holiday, bored to tears or totally uninterested. We are using this time to think about other topics, plan our next meeting, or think about our date that night – all while the other person is talking, and we are silent (to be fair, we are probably nodding our head vacantly as well). In fact, this isn't listening at all – and the Blue Brain will notice pretty quickly. Interestingly, while Level One

Listening can get us into trouble, it's not the one that sinks our boat. That is reserved for Level Two Listening.

2. **Level Two Listening – *Arguing*.** In this case, I am actually listening to you – but with an agenda. What I'm listening for is very specific – I'm listening for information, for ammunition to use against you and to prove I'm right. I listen just long enough to say, "Ha! Gotcha! That's where you're wrong!" I am listening, but only listening to argue, not to engage.

   Level Two Listening is incredibly destructive to a relationship, to true problem solving. It is actually the most significantly self-defeating tool we can use. It's like using poisoned bait. The reason is simple, as we noted in the last chapter – Newton's Third Law of Motion:

### For every Action, there is an Equal, and *Opposite*, Reaction.

Simply put, arguing – even silently arguing in our head – has the same result as aggressive telling, and telling takes us right back to hunting. When I start to argue, I am often causing you to argue as well. So I end up creating the very resistance I say I want to avoid. I end up making my own job harder and harder. Good thinking.

To truly engage the Blue Brain, to reel them in and keep the Red Brain quietly napping, we need to engage them with Level Three Listening.

3. **Level Three Listening – *Insight*.** This level is actually simple – it is listening to their Blue Brain with the intent of actually understanding what they are saying, what is important to them, and why. It consists of clarifying, summarizing or paraphrasing to confirm we understand. It consists of actions like acknowledging and validating what the Blue Brain is saying so it knows it's been heard.

Remember the strongest bait, the emotional interests? Being heard and understood, having someone acknowledge what we think or feel, is almost irresistible to us. By actively practicing Level Three Listening, you will engage in Blue Brains by the school, the shoal, the mob, the family and the pod.

## SUMMARY

> **LESSON 2**

### Baiting the Hook, Casting, and Reeling

So, back to basics. We shift from hunting to BrainFishing. From telling to asking. And we ask questions that attract and engage the Blue Brain by baiting the hook with the single most interesting and attractive thing there is for them – their own interests. We make sure we choose our bait wisely. Know what kind of bait, what kind of interests, you are working with – results (good), process (even stronger), and emotion (the strongest). The more attractive the questions you cast their way, the more engaged the other person will be. Ideally, we work with all three kinds of interests, all the time.

Once you bait and cast, you reel in Blue Brains by listening. But not any old listening, not Level One or Level Two Listening, but Level Three Listening, listening to truly understand. Engage them by giving them the interests we all most want – being heard, being acknowledged and understood.

Once you have baited the hook, cast it, and reeled in the Blue Brains with real listening, you're ready to use some of the more advanced skills and tools to keep the Blue Brains working and problem solving with you.

> **EXERCISE #2**

## Questions and the Three Types of Interests

So let's try chumming the waters a bit here. For the next important conversation you have, deliberately ask questions aimed at all three types of interests. You'll have to adapt these questions to the circumstances, but that won't be hard to do.

### Baiting the Hook and Casting Exercise:[10]

1. **Result Questions:**

   * Think of a situation you need to address. Write three questions that ask the other person about the results they want, what other outcomes might work, what options they see for solving this.

2. **Process Questions:**

   * Think about the process, structure, or framework – the context that this is taking place in. Write three questions that get their thoughts on how fair the process is, how decisions will be made, what other information would be helpful, what they like about the context or framework you're both working in.

3. **Emotion Questions:**

   * Think about how they might be feeling. Write three questions that focus on how they feel, what they see as important, how they feel they've been treated, what they see as respectful in the situation.

Keep an eye on the level of thinking and engagement you get with each type of question, and where each type of question directs or focuses the conversation.

Finally, consider starting a "Journal of Questions" to capture some of these for use in other situations you'll come across in the future.

---

10  Just a reminder, in the final section "BrainFishing Worksheets," you'll find all these exercises with plenty of space to actually do the work. Check it out!

### Three Levels of Listening

After asking some of the questions above, deliberately try out the three levels of listening:

1. **Level One: The Lights are On, But No One Is Home**

   - After they talk for a bit, suddenly look at them and say, "Sorry, did you say something?" Much fun ensues.

2. **Level Two: Attack of the Killer Red Brains**

   - We have already tried this. Listen for a bit, and then argue with them. Tell them why they are wrong. Use their own words against them to show you were "listening". Even more fun ensues.

3. **Level Three: Blue Brain Understanding**

   - This is the important exercise. Start by asking a few questions to clarify. Paraphrase what they've said, and ask if you heard it right. Acknowledge that what they've said is important. And watch carefully for their level of engagement, satisfaction, and willingness to continue talking. You've landed a Blue Brain!

## FISH STORIES — "Hide and Seek"

An employee called her HR consultant, saying she wanted to file a harassment complaint. The consultant, skilled in BrainFishing, focused on questions, and on her interests. He asked what the issue was, and what was going on. The employee unburdened herself, describing months of feeling demeaned by a co-worker, saying that the co-worker, who is young and new to the team, didn't understand this workplace, didn't listen to her even though she had much more experience, laughed in team meetings when she spoke, and was always gossiping with co-workers about her. She was clearly stressed, feeling put down and disrespected.

The HR consultant listened, mentally reaching for the paperwork to fill out a harassment complaint. Just before he went down that path, he decided to go a bit deeper by engaging the employee's Blue Brain a bit more.

Once she stopped to take a breath, he asked, "What do you see as the biggest problem you face in all of this?" The question made the employee stop and think. After a moment, she said, "My supervisor. She's the problem. She won't do anything to address this. It isn't my co-worker's fault at all – she is new and is listening to the wrong people. She doesn't know any better. Someone has to manage her!"

The consultant paused, and then asked, "How much of this have you shared with your supervisor?" The employee paused even longer. "I haven't," she said, "She's not very approachable. I know I should, but I haven't." The consultant followed with, "What help would you need to sit down with your supervisor and explain what's going on for you?"

The employee sighed, paused, and said, "You're right, I guess I should do that. But if she doesn't help me, I'll be back!" "I'll be here if you need any help," the consultant said, as he tucked the complaint paperwork away.

**BrainFishing Analysis:** *Until we ask a few questions, we really don't know what the problem is, or what the other person really needs. It's often called "shooting in the dark." After asking a few questions, actually listening can help you get to the root cause of the issue, and help you find far better solutions for the situation.*

### Filling Your Tackle Box

Okay, this is the big one. Once you've become skilled at shifting to questions, baiting your questions effectively with interests that appeal to the other Blue Brain, casting these questions into the conversation, and reeling them in by being genuinely curious and listening, you can start to refine your technique significantly.

In other words, there are a number of different types of questions you can start to try out, to apply in specific situations you face. This is your metaphorical "tackle box", and we're going to stock it with some of the most useful questioning skills and tools that there are.

To be clear, there are likely an infinite number of question types out there, many of them subtle variations on the main types of questions we'll be sharing with you here. When you become skilled at BrainFishing, you'll develop and hone your own. If you stick with it, you'll begin to find the questions that work best for you, in your line of work and in your life. We know that will happen. For now, we want you to start with the ones we have found that work, and work well.

## The Tools and Skills of Engagement

Your new tackle box, like a real fishing tackle box, has those cool trays that fold out once you open the lid. Each tray represents specific types of questions, tools, or skills you can use as the situation warrants.

The tackle box we offer you has three distinct trays, three different types of tools and skills you will find useful. They break down like this:

Level One: **First Tray – Open Questions:** Level One is the first tray, and contains three different types of open questions that accomplish engagement in different ways. We'll look at key open questions like

Information Gathering questions, Problem Solving questions, and Reality Changing questions. We'll also show you how to move from a clarifying statement to asking a powerful follow-on question. These are fundamental types of open questions which you will use a lot.

**LEVEL ONE**
**First Tray – Open Questions:**

* Information Gathering
* Problem Solving
* Reality Changing
* Statement-to-Question

Level Two: **Second Tray – Statements:** Level Two contains a small number of tools that help attract the Blue Brain in a different way – they actually tranquillize the Red Brain, calming it down so that the Blue Brain is free to stay and play. These special phrases are called Acknowledging and Empathy Statements. You do not want to go BrainFishing without these handy.

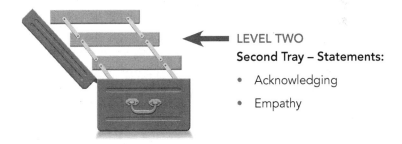

**LEVEL TWO**
**Second Tray – Statements:**

* Acknowledging
* Empathy

**Level Three: Third Tray – Miscellaneous Tools:** Level Three is a smaller tray with a few unique questions and phrases that smooth the problem solving path for everyone, and help bring resolution and closure to the problem solving process. This tray has two specific types of closed questions you will find useful in specific situations, along with some Magic Words.

**LEVEL THREE**
**Third Tray – MiscellaneousTools:**

- Asking Permission Questions
- Confirming/Closing Questions
- Magic Words

All of the important skills, tools, lures and approaches to make you a champion BrainFisher are in one of these three trays. As you'll see, we will be bouncing between the trays as we try out all the bright, shiny new toys in the tackle box.

## Level One:
## Open Questions that Gather Information

Questions that gather information are some of the safest and most useful questions there are. These are the questions to use first in many cases. Asking questions that gather information calls out to the Blue Brain, they are a siren song that will make the Blue Brain curious at first, and make you irresistible next. To draw out a Blue Brain, to let them know you are interested in hearing from them, to signal that you're fishing and not hunting, Information Gathering questions (IG) are an effective way to engage the best part of the other brain.

Information Gathering questions mostly start with result interests, asking the other person for information about the problem, the situation, or the circumstances. We ask the other party to explain and educate us. We ask for information that will eventually help us solve the problem. In reality, however, what makes Information Gathering questions effective is that they rely heavily on the strongest bait – emotional interests. In other words, what is attracting the Blue Brain is the emotional interest of being heard. All Blue Brains want to be heard, to be understood, to present their case, to have their interests on the table. These IG questions have a powerful attraction, one most Blue Brains can't resist.

Most Information Gathering questions are pretty simple to use (if not always easy). Here's a few to consider adding to your new tackle box:

### Table 4: Information Gathering Questions

| Information Gathering Question: | Reason you might ask: |
| --- | --- |
| What are the issues you've been trying to resolve? | Helps you to understand the problem. |
| How often is this happening? | More understanding the problem. |
| What's the reason you don't want to work with Fred? | Really understand the problem. |
| In your view, when should we start this project? | Taps into their knowledge to solve the problem. |
| Tell me more about that... | While technically not a question, this is one of the most effective ways to gather and solicit more information. |

Information Gathering questions are simple and direct. Ask them early, ask them often. They will provide you with an understanding of the depth, breadth and urgency behind the other person's thinking. IG questions are really the price of admission to the fishing derby.

Information Gathering questions do more than just gather information and begin to attract the Blue Brain. In most difficult situations, you don't really start talking to the Blue Brain, you first talk to the official "bouncer" at the door, the Red Brain. Remember, the Red Brain pays no attention at all to the Blue Brain's interests. It focuses on building a strong and well-fortified position as a way to keep itself safe. Red Brains, in other words, are the defenders at the gate. They tell you their position, their answer, their solution to the problem, and fully expect you to push back, to fight, and to argue – or to give in and go away. Red Brains love either outcome. It gives their existence meaning.

Information Gathering questions help you get past the Red Brain. By posing questions, by asking for information, for reasons, for the "why" behind those positions, and by side-stepping the argument and the fight, the Red Brain gets confused, unsure what to do next. It has no choice but to get some help from the Blue Brain, who, of course, is eavesdropping from not far away.

Information Gathering questions make it safe for the Blue Brain to engage. IG questions, asked with curiosity and patience, will circumvent the Red Brain and its aggressive or positional behaviour and will invite the all-important Second Shift to occur. Information Gathering questions are the basis for this shift.

We have talked about the First Shift, our shift to questions – questions with genuine curiosity, questions without judgment, open questions. And when we make the First Shift, when we ask a few Information Gathering questions to start the discussion, we start the Second Shift in the other party.

In almost every case, the first step into BrainFishing is your ability and willingness to ask good Information Gathering questions early in the discussion. Here is a deeper example:

*An employee is a day late delivering a report on a recent service issue to his manager. The manager approaches the employee to talk. This can go either down the hunting path, or the BrainFishing path. Take a look at each.*

## HUNTING:

**Manager:** "I'm very disappointed! You were supposed to have that report done by yesterday. You know I'm under pressure on this one! (*Tell, Tell, and Tell*)

**Employee:** Hey, it wasn't my fault, I'm still waiting for information from Fred, go talk to him! (*Deny, and Tell*)

**Manager:** No, you are supposed to make this happen. That was *your* job. I'm holding you accountable. (*Tell, Tell and Tell*)

**Employee:** Hold anything you want, it's not my problem. Why are you picking on me? (*Tell and Deny, with no solution in sight. And now it's getting personal.*)

## BRAINFISHING:

**Manager:** Hi, what's the status of that report? (*IG Question*)

**Employee:** Yeah, it's not ready, I'm still waiting for information from Fred. (*Tell*)

**Manager:** That's frustrating. When do you expect to get the information from Fred? (*Level 2 Acknowledging, then an IG question*)

**Employee:** It is! But I have no idea, he isn't answering my emails. (*Tell*)

**Manager:** What part of the report can you finalize without that information? (*A deeper IG question*)

**Employee:** Well, I guess I could send you all of it but the last part, would that help? (*Tell, Closed Question*)

**Manager:** It would, thanks, when can I get that? (*Level 2 Acknowledging (see Tray Two, final IG question*)

**Employee:** I'll send it now. (*Problem partly solved, moving ahead*)

**Manager:** Great. How can I help you get that information from Fred? (*Problem Solving question – see below*)

On the hunting side, the tension intensifies and escalates – both dig in and little is accomplished.

On the BrainFishing side, when the manager simply shifts from judgment to curiosity, when she focuses on Information Gathering questions rather than telling and judging, both parties engage and lean toward solving the problem rather than attacking and defending. And the employee, clearly defensive to start, de-escalates and starts solving the problem as well.

The Information Gathering questions on the BrainFishing side are questions that open the door to soliciting, collecting or requesting information. These Information Gathering questions serve to create mutual engagement and learning (Blue Brain specialties), and to move the focus away from finger pointing, justifying and blaming (Red Brain specialties).

Information Gathering questions are the foundation of BrainFishing, the fork in the road toward BrainFishing and away from hunting. That's why they are the first level of your tackle box. However simple they seem, they set the stage for effective engagement.

## FISH STORIES —
### "Take Two Emails and Call Me in the Morning"

During a recent collective bargaining session, management indicated that they needed to change the three-hour call-out pay when a technician is called in outside their shift. Simply put, their collective agreement stated that whenever an employee was called out for an emergency, they had to be paid a minimum of three hours pay regardless of how long the work actually took. Management explained that due to technology, many of the automated email alerts that a technician received from the plant in the middle of the night can be reviewed remotely, from the employee's home on their computer. Lots of them require no action until the following day, so the employee received the alert, reviewed it, and went back to bed, all in about 10 minutes. The company did not want to pay them for three hours for 10 minutes of work.

Typically, this would be seen by the union as a "concession," a take-away from their members' pay. The Red Brain, hearing the suggestion, would typically react strongly.

In this case, the lead negotiator for the union was skilled at Brain-Fishing, and rather than attack, he asked a few Information Gathering questions: "Okay, let's talk about this. How often is this happening? How many callouts have you been paying for 3 hours when it only took 10 minutes? What is the overall cost to this problem?"

Management, expecting strong pushback, was surprised – not expecting the union to be open to having a reasonable discussion, they had not prepared. They said they didn't have that information with them, they'd get back them later with the data.

Later, when the union followed up for the information, the company stated, "It actually isn't as large an issue as we thought, so we don't need to change anything at this time. Thanks for hearing us out." Problem resolved without fight, flight or conflict. Information Gathering questions can change the playing field!

**BrainFishing Analysis:** *Information Gathering questions also help eliminate assumptions or confusion around the facts. They can establish a common starting point, to everyone's benefit.*

> **EXERCISE #4**

### Information Gathering Questions

*Try this for a week, everywhere in your daily life – at work, with family, with friends, with waiters, clerks, etc.*

Using the Information Gathering approach: No matter the event, the activity, the issue that you are dealing with, commit to starting everything you say with one or two IG questions. For example:

- **Waiter at the restaurant:** *Are you ready to order?*
  **You:** *What's good here? What would you recommend?*

- **Co-worker:** *This report is taking forever to finish!*
  **You:** *What part is taking the longest? What would help?*

- **Manager:** *I need this problem addressed immediately!*
  **You:** *What's your deadline for this? What else could I put on hold to get this done?*

Give this a try. See what happens when you make the First Shift on your end, and start to make them think by engaging their Blue Brain with Information Gathering questions instead of triggering their Red Brain with statements. This approach should be your staple as a successful BrainFisher.

## Still From Level One:
## Open Questions that Focus on Problem Solving

Problem Solving (PS) questions are more concentrated and potent questions than simple IG questions. Once you have more information and some insight into the issue or problem, and once the other party is leaning in the Blue Brain direction, you can use questions to focus toward problem solving and solutioning (who invented *that* word?). Solutions give people hope; they give us a light at the end of the tunnel instead of just fighting in the dark. Problem Solving questions can be used to channel and guide the Blue Brains in the room toward something constructive while gently holding the Red Brain at bay.

Another way to think of Problem Solving questions is this. Arguing, fighting and blaming are all focused on what has already happened – who did what to cause this problem, who made this worse, who did what in the past. Human beings love to argue about the past. It is probably the most popular hobby in the world, beating philately (yeah, stamp collecting) by a country mile. The problem is this – there are no problems that can be solved in the past. None. Only argument, blame and disengagement lie that way. All problems are solved in the present, looking forward into the future. Problem Solving questions focus us forward rather than backward.

Take a look at a few of these:

### Table 5: Problem Solving Questions

| Problem Solving Questions: | Reason you might ask: |
| --- | --- |
| What ideas do you have to resolve this? | Solicit their ideas, and engage them in solving the problem. |
| What would happen if we tried doing "X"? | This question focuses their thinking in a very specific direction, toward a specific solution. |
| Who might have information that would help us? | This is process bait, helping them step back and think a bit more broadly about the way we are approaching the problem. |
| In your view, when would be a good time to communicate with the other team? | Tap into their knowledge to solve the problem. |
| Based your experience, how do you think we can solve this problem most effectively? | Signal to them that their point of view is important, and you want their expertise. |
| How would we avoid "X" from happening again? | Aim the problem solving at avoiding a previous failure, and keep it future-focused. |
| What is a new approach we can try on this? | Get some out-of-the-box thinking going. |

Problem Solving questions go further and deeper than the more generic Information Gathering questions, and they do more than just gather information. They help build a collaborative sense of engagement and possibility.

In most cases these two types of questions should be used in sequence – start with IG questions until you have a good sense of what is really going on, then shift to Problem Solving questions to keep the focus and momentum on solutioning (*yeesh!*).

Here's a deeper look at applying Problem Solving questions.

*Two managers are working on a project together. It's not going well.*

## HUNTING:

**Manager #1:** You know, when we started this project, we had a pretty clear plan. It's all fallen apart now. (*Tell and Judge*)

**Manager #2:** Clearly the plan wasn't good enough, look where we are. (*Judge, and Tell*)

**Manager #1:** The plan was fine, your team couldn't execute it, that's all. (*Tell, and Judge*)

**Manager #2:** Don't try and put this on us, it's your plan, we're just here to support you, if you'd let us! (*Judge and Accuse, Justify with a Tell*)

## BRAINFISHING:

**Manager #1:** So, the project isn't going very well, what do you see as the issues? (*IG question*)

**Manager #2:** Well, the project plan isn't good enough, that's clear. (*Judge and Tell*)

**Manager #1:** That might be part of the problem, I'm not sure. Where do you think we're stuck? (*Level 2 Acknowledging, then an IG question*)

**Manager #2:** We don't know what our role is on this. We're supposed to be your technology resource, but we don't see your team using us for that. (*Tell, with some good Information*)

## HUNTING:

**Manager #1:** Sorry, this is on you, you're supposed to be experts on the technology side, and we sure haven't seen any of that! (*Judge, Tell, Judge*)

**Manager #2:** We're stepping away until you get your act together. Call us when you know what you want. (*Tell, Unilateral Decision, finish with an "up yours"*)

## BRAINFISHING:

**Manager #1:** I see. Where do you see you can add value right away, given where we are today? (*First PS question*)

**Manager #2:** Well, I think we should focus on solving the bugs in the program. It has to be done at some point, why not now? (*Idea, still a bit defensive*)

**Manager #1:** I think it would be a start, thanks. If my team re-worked the project plan in the meantime, how would that help? (*Level 2 Acknowledging, PS question*)

**Manager #2:** Yes, we need that revised, immediately. (*Confirming Tell*)

**Manager #1:** Great, let's start with that. When can we meet to review progress, and keep this on track for us both? (*PS question using process interests*)

On the hunting side, notice how the judgments and the "tells" derail any creative thinking and prevent any problem solving. The telling and the judging drive both parties toward disengagement and blame. They are hunting and blaming – and it is all about the past!

On the BrainFishing side, even with Manager #2 still judging and telling at the beginning, the Information Gathering questions at the beginning (and Level 2 Acknowledging – see below), followed by focused Problem Solving questions, channel both of them back to effective engagement and toward a solution. BrainFishing with Problem Solving questions keeps everyone future-focused and deepens our Blue Brain engagement. Yup. BrainFishing.

## ➤ EXERCISE #5

### Problem Solving Questions

Build on the last Information Gathering exercise. After asking one or two IG questions, follow them with one or two Problem Solving questions. See if the other Blue Brain gets more engaged, thinks more. Note the behaviour, and see if it helps keep you both focused on solving the problem.

Examples of using Problem Solving questions:

- **Waiter at the restaurant:** *Are you ready to order?* **You:** *What's good here? What else would you recommend?* **Waiter:** *I'd recommend the steak, it's excellent!* **You:** *Thanks, I'm not a big meat eater at lunch, what would you suggest that's bit lighter? Which would you suggest, the Caesar salad, or the fish tacos?*

- **Co-worker:** *This report is taking forever to finish!* **You:** *What part is taking the longest? What would help?* **Co-worker:** *It's the amount of data, it's killing me.* **You:** *Who else might help with that? Who on the team is good with data?*

- **Manager:** *I need this problem addressed immediately!* **You:** *What's your deadline for this? What else could I put on hold to get this done?* **Manager:** *I need it by the end of the week, if you can believe that!* **You:** *If I took this on, who else could you assign to help me, so we can finish by Friday?*

Notice how Problem Solving questions flow nicely from Information Gathering questions. IG questions set the table and they bring us together in a common reality; without them, Problem Solving questions may not always engage the Blue Brains enough to land them.

## FISH STORIES — "What Do *You* Think You Should Do?"

A manager in the commercial loans department of a major bank was drowning in work. One thing that took up an inordinate amount of time in his day was when his direct reports would come in and ask him to solve a problem for them – what reports to file; how to write up a risk evaluation; reviewing collateral issues; advice on how to talk to a difficult client, etc. all day long. He wanted be a good manager and was a genuinely and sincerely helpful person – but he was drowning.

He decided he needed to try something different. When the next person entered his office he would simply ask them, "What do you think you should do?" And then he would shut up and listen to their answer. Minutes later, the first employee walked in with a request. He asked his problem solving question. Surprisingly, the employee had a suggestion – a very good idea, in fact – and the manager told them so: "That sounds great. Let me know how it turns out." The employee left with a broad smile on her face. So he tried it with the next request...and the next...and the next. "What do you think you should do?" followed by Level Three Listening to understand.

Occasionally – very rarely – he had to ask a follow up question or two, but usually his people – smart, hardworking, well-trained – had very good answers. The meetings went fast and everyone was more satisfied. A great outcome, but then it got even better! In the following weeks, the manager realized that his staff was coming to him less and less frequently. He had more time to concentrate on other work, the department was getting more work done, and more loans were getting processed than ever before. One day, he asked one of his staff what was happening, why she didn't come in as often to ask for his help and she told him, "Well, I knew you were going to ask me, 'What do you think you should do?' so I just started asking it of myself and realized I knew the answer most of the time. It was faster and easier to just think about it, and do it. I still bring you the difficult issues, but I'm getting way more done."

*BrainFishing Analysis: When you tell people the answer, at best you get compliance. When you ask people for their thoughts and input, you get commitment. You make full use of their knowledge and experience, while at the same time showing respect and deepening trust. Engaging people into the problem solving process benefits everyone involved.*

## Next Up – Level Two:
## Acknowledging and Empathy

As you saw in some of the examples above, Acknowledging/Empathy (AE) statements can play an effective role in BrainFishing. A critical part of the engagement process is to send an advance team to pave the way, to smooth the waters to help make BrainFishing more effective. We do this with Acknowledging/Empathy statements. AE statements interrupt any negative emotions in the Red Brain, de-escalate negative reactions, and help the Blue Brain focus and pay attention. They cause the other person to actually listen. While Information Gathering and Problem Solving questions can often engage the Blue Brain, there are times when the Red Brain does not give up so easily – especially in difficult or high conflict situations.

Remember, the Red Brain's sole job is to protect the castle, to fend off attacks and keep the Blue Brain safe. It takes this job very, very seriously.

Because of this, it can take more than simply asking questions to calm it down. After all, we've already seen where ineffective questions can be used to judge and to blame.

Acknowledging/Empathy statements take many forms, including recognizing, validating, and of course, acknowledging. These statements convey to the Red Brain that we are taking them seriously, we don't think they're stupid, wrong, or crazy, and that we see their point of view as important. Being taken seriously tames the wild beast in all of us pretty quickly.

Take a look at a few of these.

### Table 6: Acknowledging/Empathy Statements

| Provocative Red Brain Statements: | Typical Responses that Escalate the Red Brain: | Level 2 AE, plus IG or PS Questions: |
| --- | --- | --- |
| *There's only one solution to this – mine!* | *No way, that simply won't work, it will fail!* | **You're obviously committed to that approach.** *How exactly would that solution work?* |
| *That's my job, not yours. You need to stop interfering!* | *Who do you think you are!? That's always been part of my job!* | **You see this as your responsibility, and I'm certainly not trying to take over.** *What approach might work for us both?* |
| *We keep telling you this doesn't work for us, and you keep ignoring us!* | *We only ignore what isn't relevant!* | **So, that's clearly important, and it's not working for you.** *What exactly do you think I'm missing here?* |

Notice how in each case simply refuting or arguing will just escalate the situation. By inserting a direct, simple Acknowledging/Empathy statement before asking a question, it calms the Red Brain enough for their Blue Brain to actually hear the question.

In some cases, the Red Brain is so upset, angry and protective, it may take a minute or two of doing nothing but listening and acknowledging before the Red Brain can relax enough for the Blue Brain to come out and play. Be patient. There are no "recipes" here, such that one or two AE statements will always be enough. Listen and acknowledge – in words, tone and body language – until the Blue Brain shows up. That's when to shift to Information Gathering and Problem Solving questions.

And we must emphasize: unless you actually do agree with something the Red Brain is saying, *do not* confuse "acknowledging" with "agreeing". Never confuse the other Red Brain by seeming to agree when you don't. Remember, agreeing with someone can be very helpful, and we should agree with the other person wherever we actually *do* agree. But in many cases, we *don't* agree, or haven't decided if we agree or not – we haven't yet gone deep enough to understand the problem we're actually trying to solve. So we need a way to let the Red Brain know it's safe, that we take it seriously – without yet agreeing or disagreeing. If you appear to agree with the Red Brain, it may calm down at first – but you'll get double the anger from the Red Brain when it finds out later that you don't, actually, agree. Phrases that accidently convey agreement typically cause way more problems down the road.

There are a few examples of the difference:

### Table 7: Acknowledging Without Agreeing

| Statements that Agree: | Statements that Acknowledge without Agreeing: |
| --- | --- |
| I completely understand.... | I see what you're getting at... |
| You're right, I'd be upset if that happened to me, too.... | That was difficult... |
| You're right, that makes a lot of sense... | That's important, we need to talk about it... |

The statements on the left are not taken by the Red Brain as acknowledgment, but rather as confirmation that the Red Brain is *right*. It goes way beyond simply acknowledging the issues as important. The instant the Red Brain sees that you don't actually agree with everything they are saying, it will see you as untrustworthy, and you'll be stuck with the Red Brain for a long, long time. The statements on the right simply acknowledge something as important, difficult or understood – acknowledgement, not agreement.

### ▶ EXERCISE #6

### Acknowledging/Empathy Statements

Here is a BrainFishing practice for you to try. For the next week, start all your responses to co-workers, friends, and partners with an Acknowledging/Empathy statement before answering or asking a question. And pause ever so slightly after the AE statement for greater effect. For example:

- **Co-Worker:** *This project is driving me crazy, I can't stand it.*
  **You:** *Sounds pretty frustrating. (pause) What are you thinking of doing?*

- **Co-worker:** *How do you get the #%@*$)@! software to do this?!* **You:** *Yeah, it can be hard to figure that out. (pause) What have you tried so far? (pause) Can I show you how I approach that? (an Ask Permission question, see below.)*

- **Partner:** *You never take out the garbage!* **You:** *I know that's my responsibility. (pause) I'm home at 6, how would that work?*

Then, try it a few more times by going straight to a response, a tell. See what the reaction is, both when you start with an Acknowledging/ Empathy statement, and when you go straight to a tell. See how much time you stay with the Red Brain, and how much more quickly you're working with the Blue Brain in each case.

### FISH STORIES —
### "You've Had a Hard Day. Anything I Can Do to Help?"

On a business trip to Europe, a business traveller was checking in. The agent was clearly having a bad, bad day — stressed, and muttering to himself. "Tough day?" asked the traveller. "You don't know the half of it!" fumed the agent, typing heavily on the computer. "I've been here 10 hours, and they've told me I have to cover another four hours! And with the delays today, I've put up with nothing but abuse!" "That's lousy, it does sound like a hard day at the office!" said the traveller. "Anything I can do to help?" "Wish you could," laughed the agent. "I can't even get you an aisle seat, like you requested!" "No worries," said the traveller, "I appreciate you trying." The agent paused, and looked at the traveller. "You're the nicest guy I've had this whole shift," he said. "You know what, business class has an aisle seat open. I've just upgraded you!"

*BrainFishing Analysis:* Acknowledging/Empathy statements often trigger reciprocal actions from the other party – they often acknowledge in return. Use them often!

## Back to Level One:
## Open Questions that Challenge or Change Reality

Reality Changing (RC) questions are some of the most powerful and advanced questions you can use; they take the most skill as well. Once you are comfortable shifting from hunting to fishing, to asking Information Gathering questions and Problem Solving questions while slipping in Level 2 AE statements when needed, you're ready to engage some of the trickiest Blue Brains, to draw them in and keep them working through the most difficult conversations you can imagine.

Using just Information Gathering and Problem Solving questions can often get you where you need to go. But sometimes, after gathering good information, and after focusing the process on problem solving, we still hit a snag. Even though we have engaged that other Blue Brain, it may turn out that the other Blue Brain is just, well, *wrong.* Or misguided. Or seeing the problem from an unrealistic point of view. Or working from a set of interests that is preventing you both from finding a solution. In this case, we may have to challenge or help to change their perspective.

Reality Changing questions can help you engage Blue Brains in difficult conversations while minimizing the risk of the Red Brain suddenly jumping in to derail everything. They also help us keep our own Blue Brains engaged, and prevent our own Red Brain from jumping in to judge, to lecture, or to argue. Many times it's not their Red Brain that's the problem, it's ours!

Here's another way to look at this. It turns out that there are two fundamental reasons for asking questions:

- **Asking Questions – Reason #1:** The first one is obvious – it's to gather information. Information Gathering questions do that, and do it well. Open, non-judgmental questions, as we saw, calm the Red Brain, engage the Blue Brain, and gain us (and them) valuable information that helps with the move toward problem solving. Problem Solving questions take us even deeper, helping us to gather useful information and develop solutions to the problem we're facing. This is all good. In both cases, we ask IG questions and PS questions to get better information and ideas on the table.

- **Asking Questions – Reason #2:** The second reason to ask questions, however, is not to *gather* information, but *to convey information*, or to cause the other Blue Brain to think about implications or consequences that they may not like or want, or simply have not considered as possibilities. They may be avoiding difficult situations. They may be in flat out denial about them. When you've asked IG and PS questions effectively, and you and the other Blue Brain still disagree, only one of two things can happen. Either we both call up the Red Brains and go back to battling it out winner-take-all style, or we engage even more deeply, challenge each other's thinking, drill even further into Blue Brain territory. To accomplish the latter, we sometimes have to "make" or "cause" the other party to think differently about the problem. To help them see it from another point of view. Reality Changing questions can actually take the other person out of denial and cause them to see the problem quite differently.

When faced with a Blue Brain that is stuck in one place and one point of view, when it can't seem to move forward, it takes a special kind of skill to fundamentally shift that situation, to re-direct the trajectory of the conversation – in effect, to change the existing "reality".

Take a look at this:

## Table 8: **Reality Changing Questions**

| Reality Changing Questions: | Reason you might ask: |
|---|---|
| *If we don't resolve this situation, where do you see it going from here?* | This challenges them to think about the consequences, instead of just focusing on the problem. |
| *We can both take this to the courts. How many years are you thinking it will take before we get an answer, and how much do you think we'll both spend?* | This moves the focus beyond the result interests to include the process interests, making us both think about the problem a bit differently – if not necessarily happily. |
| *How would you assess your level of productivity compared to the rest of the team?* | This question makes them see their work performance from a different context. |
| *If your productivity doesn't improve, what do you think will happen, and happen quickly?* | This question points sharply to some very negative consequences. |
| *Assuming you win this lawsuit, how much business do you think we will do with your company in the future?* | This again makes the other party think about the consequences, not just about winning. |
| *Based on our discussions, what solutions do you see that might work for both of us?* | This starts to change their reality and focus from their interests alone, to a more common set of Interests. |
| *If you don't change this behaviour, how long do you think the company will keep you here?* | This is a very strong RC question, making the other brain think deeply about ultimate consequences. |

Reality Changing questions can be tough and direct. Because of this, RC questions must also be asked with deep curiosity and minimal judgment. You must be very clear in your own Blue Brain that your intention is to create a win-win solution. This is why intention is such an important part of BrainFishing. In asking someone to consider shifting the way they think about the world and their interests, you are asking them to – literally – change their reality. Reality Changing questions must be asked in an open, neutral way in order to minimize this being seen as an attack or a threat. In addition, dipping frequently into Level 2 – Acknowledging/Empathy statements is a must when you use RC questions, as you'll see below.

Make no mistake, Reality Changing questions can drill to the heart of the issue quickly. They put the other Blue Brain under pressure, paint a picture the other Blue Brain may not like. But they do so with the minimum level of resistance, with as little telling, arguing or fighting as is possible. When successful, they keep the difficult conversation in the land of the Blue Brain and prevent a reversion to Red Brain behaviour.

It is important to note that RC questions are *not* intended to trick or to force the other brain to agree with you, or give you the answer you want. Not at all. They do the important work of making the other person see the situation differently, actually consider other points of view, other consequences that may not have been thought of. In the end, it's still their call and their decision. But it helps the other Blue Brain discover, for itself, that change is necessary. And when the other person sees and understands another point of view clearly, different and better outcomes are not far behind.

Here's a deeper look at applying Reality Changing questions.

*Two managers are working on a project together. It's really, really, really not going well.*

## HUNTING:

**Manager #1:** You know, when we started this project, we had a pretty clear plan. It's all fallen apart now. (*Tell and Judge*)

**Manager #2:** Clearly, the plan wasn't good enough, look where we are. (*Judge, and Tell*)

**Manager #1:** The plan was fine, your team couldn't execute it, that's all. (*Tell, and Judge*)

**Manager #2:** My team! I resent that! I think it's time I talk to the Vice-president, I've had enough. (*Judge and Threaten*)

**Manager #1:** I don't care what you do, I've already spoken to the Vice-president, he knows who's responsible for what, believe me. (*Dismiss, Tell, Judge*)

**Manager #2:** So you went behind my back and smeared my name, great! That's harassment and bullying! I'll put an end to that right away! (*Accuse, Threaten and Threaten*)

## BRAINFISHING:

**Manager #1:** So, the project isn't going very well, what do you see as the issues? (*IG Question*)

**Manager #2:** Well, the project plan isn't good enough, that's clear. (*Judge and Tell*)

**Manager #1:** That might be part of the problem, I'm not sure. Where do you think we're stuck? (*Acknowledging/Empathy statement, then an IG question*)

**Manager #2:** We don't know what our role is on this. We're supposed to be your technology resource, but we don't see your team using us for that. (*Tell, with good Information*)

**Manager #1:** I see. Where do you see your team can add value right away, given where we are today? (*First PS question*)

**Manager #2:** I don't know. I don't see how we can fix this. (*Tell, refuse to problem solve*)

| HUNTING: | BRAINFISHING: |
|---|---|
| | **Manager #1:** Well, if your team focused on bug fixes for the next week while we revised the project plan, what would you think of that approach? (*More direct and focused PS question*) |
| | **Manager #2:** I don't think that will work, no. I'm not going to throw more resources at this problem. (*Stuck, refusing to move*) |
| | **Manager #1:** We do seem stuck. If I propose the idea I just mentioned to the Vice-president, how would you feel about that? (*RC question*) |
| | **Manager #2:** Wait a minute, that doesn't seem right, are you trying find a way to blame us for this? (*Reaction, Closed question*) |
| | **Manager #1:** Not at all, I'm hoping we can figure this out together. I'm just worried about senior management on this. What will happen if our teams can't deliver on this project? (*AE Statement, followed by another RC question.*) |
| | **Manager #2:** This won't look good for either of us, that's pretty clear. |
| | **Manager #1:** If going to the VP right now doesn't work for you, what other ideas do you have to help us move the project forward? (*AE Statement, back to PS question*) |

| HUNTING: | BRAINFISHING: |
|---|---|

**Manager #2:** I don't think bug fixes are the best thing right now, but what if my team reviewed the deliverables to see if there's a better approach? (*Denial to Save Face, Idea*)

**Manager #1:** Actually, that might work well. My team can draft a new project plan, and review it with you once your team has reviewed the deliverables, how is that? (*Level 2 Acknowledgment, confirm the way forward*)

**Manager #2:** Okay, let's get some dates nailed down.

On the hunting side, it can devolve quickly into threats and reciprocal threats – your basic tit-for-tat. Both managers will feel justified and self-righteous. This will be followed by multiple meetings, escalations, and further arguments. The short conversation above does not indicate a fast resolution at all. And the project will suffer, big time.

On the BrainFishing side, even when Manager #2 digs her heels in and initially refuses to problem solve, the two Reality Changing questions shift her reality, challenge it just enough to loosen up the problem solving process. That's what good Reality Changing questions can do for you. Put a few of these into practice, and see what happens!

### FISH STORIES — "Tear a Strip Off This..."

A few years ago, a senior manager, with way too much signing authority at his firm, was fond of frequenting "gentlemen's clubs." One evening, he met an exotic dancer at the club, and they started an affair. Their affair lasted about a year, in total. He was so smitten that he showered her with cash and gifts (from the company coffers) totalling approximately $800,000, bankrupting the company he worked for in the process. He went to prison for his efforts. The bankruptcy receiver tried to re-claim the gifts the manager had bestowed on the dancer – legally, she was not entitled to keep them, even though she had done nothing wrong. The problem was this: since she was married and her husband had a good income, the money and gifts she had received had been co-mingled with the couple's assets, making it very hard to quantify.

At the mediation, the receivers told the mediator that they had documents that could clearly identify only about $150,000 of the money she had received, and that's what they were trying to collect. Knowing they may not get all $150,000, their bottom line to collect and settle the case was $100,000. The dancer and her husband didn't want to pay anything, but managed to agree on offering $75,000 to make this lawsuit go away. They hit an impasse at those numbers.

The husband was angry and upset – and deeply in denial. He kept saying that his wife had not received any money from the manager and that his wife had never even met the man, and he went ballistic whenever any reference to an affair was raised. The dancer recognized that the more money she suggested they pay to settle the lawsuit, the more her husband took it as an indication that she had indeed cheated on him – and received money, to boot.

In the final meeting, the dancer and her husband both refused to pay a penny more than $75,000. The other side had made it clear that unless it was $100,000, they would proceed to a trial. The mediator, in the room with the dancer, her husband and her lawyer, worked them through this:

| Mediator Dialogue: | BrainFishing Skills and Tools Used: |
|---|---|
| **Mediator:** So, it looks like we're stuck. They have indicated that their final offer is $100,000, or they have to go to court. What are your thoughts on that? | Information Gathering question. |
| **Husband:** No way, we'll never pay that! We didn't get any of this money! Everything we have, I've worked hard for! This is a scam, we're not paying! | Red Brain freewheelin' it! |
| **Mediator:** We've all looked at your bank statements, they show significant increases over this time period which you haven't been able to explain. What will happen if you can't find the documentation on where that money came from? | Reality Changing question. |
| **Husband:** It's none of their business where it came from! | Red Brain – deep in denial. |
| **Mediator:** I know your privacy is an issue here, for sure. (To the dancer) What are your thoughts on this? | Acknowledging/ Empathy statement, followed by an IG question. |
| **Dancer:** It's not fair, I just want this all to end! I'm the victim here! | Red Brain denial, anger. |

| Mediator Dialogue: | BrainFishing Skills and Tools Used: |
|---|---|
| **Husband:** Tell them $75,000 is all they'll get, and convince them to take it! | Red Brain to Power, trying to force a solution. |
| **Mediator:** I wish I could. I have tried, and they are stuck on $100,000, I'm afraid. | AE statement. |
| **Mediator:** Well, I think we're just stuck. You feel victimized by this, and you don't want to pay more than $75,000. You want to be left alone, and you want your privacy respected. They, on the other hand believe you received over $800, 000. They are only willing to settle for a minimum of $100,000. | AE, AE, AE statements. |
| **Mediator:** When parties feel this strongly about all these issues, perhaps the best path is to simply go to court, where everyone will get to tell their story. You will get to deny everything they say, and will have the chance to show all of your financials for the last five years, in detail, to prove it. They will also be able to look at all your financials in great detail. Plus, the embezzler will have the chance to tell the story of the | Short Tell to set up the Reality Changing questions at the end. |

| Mediator Dialogue: | BrainFishing Skills and Tools Used: |
|---|---|
| affair, the cash, and the gifts, start to finish. And since it will be in open court, open to the public, everyone will know the truth. | |
| Mediator: So, how do you both feel about the opportunity to tell your story publicly, to prove you are right in open court – compared to having this all go away today for that additional $25,000 and no further legal fees? Which of these work best for you? | RC questions, going to the core of the issue. |
| Husband (after a long, painful pause): God D#%&$*! Pay the SOB's the $100,000 and let's get out of here! | Having looked at the reality posed by the RC questions, the Husband re-thinks what he insisted would never change. |

BrainFishing Analysis: *Reality Changing questions make the other party see the problem from a different point of view. They literally* **help** *them to see the situation differently, and when anyone sees a situation differently, they frequently change their actions or decisions.*

## Changing Reality with Reality Changing Questions

Practicing with Reality Changing questions requires more thought and preparation than with Information Gathering or Problem Solving questions. They work best in situations where you feel stuck, where you are getting resistance, or where you have "solved" something more than a few times, and it doesn't seem to stay solved. That is when to pull out the RC tool. Follow this process to create effective Reality Changing questions:

### How to Chart Reality Changing Questions:

#1: Identify what you want to convey, or what you want them to have to consider and think about. Be specific:

#2: Identify *their* Interests – what impacts them, what do they want, what are they afraid of around this issue:

#3: Based on the above information, prepare questions that you can ask that will cause them to see reality differently, see consequences they have been ignoring, or see the problem from a different angle:

So, find a situation that has been a bit of a challenge, or one that has not stayed solved. Before you talk to the other person, write out two or three RC questions you may need to ask, following the process above. As you talk with them, ask a couple RC questions – combined with Information Gathering questions if needed. Remember – be curious, not judgmental! Be in your Blue Brain and watch for telltale signs of their Blue Brain swimming deeper into thought – pausing, looking upward as they think, listening a bit more, etc. This means "reality" is perhaps changing a bit.

## More Reality Changing Questions:
## Take it Even Deeper with "What If" Questions

One particularly useful – and easy – type of Reality Changing question is called a "hypothetical" or What If (WI) question. These are still a type of Reality Changing question, but they follow a simple pattern that accomplishes Reality Changing quite effectively.

Consider a few of these:

### Table 8: What If (WI) Reality Changing Questions

| What If Questions: | Reason you might ask: |
| --- | --- |
| If we don't get any more resources on this project, what do you think the chances of finishing it on time are? | Their brain probably answers with a loud "NONE!" in their head, even before they speak. |
| If you win the $100k you are suing for, but it costs you over $120k to actually win this, what do you see as the purpose of the lawsuit? | This question paints the painful picture of a "no win" situation, and makes them consider it directly. |
| Assuming for a moment we accept your proposal, how does that address the important concerns we have raised with you? | This question makes the other party see the issue from your point of view, actually think about the solution from something other than their own perspective. |
| If our concerns aren't addressed, what are the chances the members will ratify this deal? | This is an extension of the last question, and forces the other party to confront the fact that unless both concerns are addressed, there won't be a deal. |

What If questions are some of the best Reality Changing questions around, and generate the minimum level of resistance even as they directly challenge the other party's views. It keeps the Blue Brain deeply engaged, even when the going gets tough.

> **EXERCISE #8**

**Changing More Reality With What If Questions**

Look for a situation where there is a history of Red Brain behaviour – of arguing, resisting, debating, etc. Then, follow the Reality Changing question three-step process above and write two or three RC or What If questions. Give them a try. After you ask one, listen carefully to the response, and ask them about their response – a good follow on question. See what happens. Then answer the following questions:

1. What happened when you asked a Reality Changing or a What If question?

2. Did you see signs of them having to think, or re-think, e.g. pausing to consider, looking up and away for a moment, starting and stopping in their response, expressing some new uncertainty, even acknowledging some of the new focus you brought to the situation? Watch for these and don't miss them – The Blue Brain is re-thinking![11]

## More Reality Changing Skills: **Statement-to-Question**

There is one more type of Reality Changing question that can also be effective in shaping difficult conversations with Blue Brains. There are times, for example, when going directly to RC questions is not appropriate. When you need to convey specific information to the other party before you

---

11  We love homework – especially this kind. As a homework assignment, watch a few episodes of the old TV show *Columbo*, starring Peter Falk. The show is a master class in asking all of these different kinds of questions, with Columbo regularly using them to get the murderers to talk themselves right into confessing. It was only years later that we realized this wasn't a series of true crime documentaries…

engage their thinking, going directly to Reality Changing questions may not succeed. You sometimes need to get important data on the table first.

In these circumstances, it only makes sense to convey that information first. To actually tell the other party what they need to hear *before* engaging them with questions. You heard right – there are times when a "tell" is quite appropriate.

First, a caution. Whenever deciding to tell someone some information, there are a few hard and fast rules. First, keep it short and to the point. You have a maximum of about two sentences before they tune out and stop listening, or in the worst case, start to argue with you – externally or internally. So keep it short and sweet.

Secondly, the approach to use is this: a combination of a statement that is immediately followed by a question. A Statement-to-Question (STQ). It can be a Statement-to-Information Gathering question, it can be a Statement-to-Problem Solving question, or a Statement-to-Reality Changing question. It's your choice; use the one that best fits the issue you're tackling. The key to all of them, however, is that there is no break between the statement and the following question.

Here are some examples of Statement-to-Question:

#### Table 9: **Statements-to-Questions**

| Statement-To-Question: | Reason to Use: |
| --- | --- |
| *That's not within our mandate – what other ways have you thought of that might help us solve this problem?* | Statement-to-Problem-Solving question. Establish that you cannot do what they're asking – but you're open to some other ideas. |
| *I don't think my client will accept that – what would you think about a different approach, like X?* | Another Statement-to-Problem-Solving question. Make it clear that their suggestion won't work – but find out what they think about *your* client's offer. |

| Statement-To-Question: | Reason to Use: |
|---|---|
| *I'm not prepared to agree to that number – if I could get close to $750,000, how interested would you be?* | Statement-to-Reality-Changing question. Directly tell them that their offer will not be acceptable – and get them focused on thinking about your counter-offer. |
| *I'm sorry, you were not the successful candidate for the promotion. When do you want to discuss the reasons for this, and how I can best support you the next time you apply for a similar position?* | Statement-to-Information-Gathering question. Communicate directly that they didn't get what they wanted and they're still valued – and find out from them what you can do to help. |

In each case, a good Statement-to-Question puts a stake in the ground by conveying a direct, clear piece of information to the other party, one that is often negative and risks throwing them back into a Red Brain reaction of fight or flight. But before their Blue Brain can leave the stage, the question engages the Blue Brain into focusing beyond the bad news, and into the interests that may keep the Blue Brain in charge and working even harder to solve the problem.

## Now Add Level Three: Closed Questions and Magic Words

We have focused on the foundational level, Level 1: Open Questions. Lots to choose from and work with there, for sure. We delved into Level 2 using Acknowledging/Empathy statements to smooth the water, to keep the Blue Brain on the line with you. Those alone will help make you a first class BrainFisher, someone skilled at deeply engaging the other party even when dealing with difficult issues.

Since we're exploring the full tackle box, the full range of questioning skills to build and support effective problem solving, there are a few other important tools and techniques that can help you deepen your skills in this process. We're now on Level 3, rummaging around a bit, and finding a couple of small but powerful additions to your tackle box that will help.

## Asking Permission Questions

Red Brains tend to have a single focus – protecting the Blue Brain. One of the best ways to do that is to attack anything that is seen to be a threat. Now, in civilized society, "attack" doesn't mean a physical attack (we hope!), it usually means the Red Brain taking an aggressive stance, blaming, pointing metaphorical fingers, dumping the problem into any lap but theirs.

One of the best ways for a Red Brain to control a conversation is to talk, and talk a lot, often without saying anything that will help solve the problem. Sometimes, we need to break that cycle to get their Blue Brain engaged and listening. One way to do that is with Asking Permission questions.

Asking Permission (AP) questions are simple, closed questions that ask permission to do something, like give an answer or explain a key point. When we actually have to tell the other person something (as we said, telling can be useful, in small quantities!), it's important that they actually hear it. But as we saw, telling is rarely successful on its own, and rarely results in the other party listening. An AP question can change that.

Quite simply, an Asking Permission question is a question that literally asks the other party permission to be told something. Notice the interests being relied upon here – how does it make you feel when someone asks you permission, rather than barging ahead without your input? It likely makes you feel respected and included. It feels like they actually care a bit about what you think or want. It recognizes your presence. This is the strongest bait – it directly meets your emotional interests of recognition and respect. As we saw, these are powerful interests. So, whenever you need to tell something to someone, Ask Permission first.

Consider a few of these:

**Table 10: Asking Permission Questions**

| Asking Permission Questions: | Reason you might ask: |
| --- | --- |
| *Is now a good time to review the cost of our proposals? Would that help?* | Gets their full attention on the cost implications of both proposals. |
| *Can I explain my reasoning for making this decision? Is now a good time?* | Signals to them there are reasons that have not been heard yet. |
| *I think it would help to look at the other issues we have to address – can we change the topic for a few minutes to put this into perspective?* | This question broadens the scope, and asks permission to change the process for a while. |
| *Can I walk you through our proposal, start to finish, before we look at what works and what doesn't?* | This gets permission to have the floor for a full presentation, without interruption. |

The value of Asking Permission questions is that they are closed questions, and therefore have only two answers – *Yes* or *No*. And either is fine. Here's why:

- **YES:** If you get a "yes" to your Asking Permission question, bonus! Since they have given you permission to do what you asked, they are likely to abide by the agreement. They will likely hear you out, listen to what you say, and follow the process you asked for – because they gave permission! This can help keep the Blue Brain completely engaged and the Red Brain quiet, because the Red Brain still feels in control – after all, it gave you permission!

- **NO:** If you get a "no", it means they are just not ready to listen yet. Had you simply gone ahead and started talking at them, they would certainly not have listened, and probably would start to argue – the Red Brain takes over and nothing you said would have helped. Whenever we get a "no" to a permission question, we simply fall back to an Information Gathering or a Problem Solving question, something like this:

  You: I had a few ideas on how to fix this, can I throw a few on the table now?
  Them: No! I don't want any more stupid ideas right now!
  You: Got it. So, what would help us solve this? What should we do next?

The Problem Solving questions you ask at the end accept that they are not ready to hear your ideas just yet, and put the ball back in their court to suggest a way forward. We're still engaged with the Blue Brain!

> **EXERCISE #9**

**Permission Questions Granted**

For the next week, try asking permission with a good Asking Permission question before just leaping ahead with your next idea. Try a few of these, adjusting them to fit the situation:

- *So, shall we start reviewing the proposals?*
- *Can we look at paragraph 12 for a minute? I think it affects our decision.*
- *Would you mind walking me through that process again, I'm not sure I got it.*
- *Can we set up a schedule for the rest of the week before we wrap this up?*
- *Can I explain our reasoning on this? Would now be a good time?*

Watch carefully for the response. Remember, ask any question, especially these, with true curiosity – with a win-win intention, not as a hidden demand or statement. And then don't assume an answer – ask, shut up, listen, and wait for the answer to come...

## Confirming/Closing Questions

Confirming/Closing (CC) questions are also closed questions that are used to literally close off the discussion and confirm the solution or next steps. They narrow the focus to ensure that both parties are actually on the same page. And they should be used only at or near the end of a topic or the end of a discussion.

Whereas Asking Permission questions are often focused on the process (asking permission for the next step, typically), Confirming/Closing questions are more content-focused, aimed at confirming the agreement itself (yes, the agreement can be on next steps, but we want you to see you can and should confirm content, too).

Consider a few of these:

### Table 11: Confirming/Closing Questions

| Confirming/Closing Questions: | Reason you might ask: |
| --- | --- |
| *Are we agreed, then, that we'll defer this topic to the next meeting?* | To confirm we're done with this item, and confirm the next step with it. |
| *So, it sounds like we're agreed on Option 2 to be implemented next week, is that right?* | Finalizing and closing off the decision. |
| *If we agree to cover the travel costs, and you pay the cost of a new computer, we'll have this settled, is that right?* | This is a fun hybrid of a What If question and a Confirming/Closing question. Wheeee! |

| Confirming/Closing Questions: | Reason you might ask: |
|---|---|
| *Just for clarity, we are both agreeing to not change any language at this time – status quo is acceptable to both parties, is that correct?* | This double checks the final agreement. |

Confirming/Closing questions are simple and direct – and indispensable. Many people engage the other Blue Brain deeply, but then assume their understanding is correct and don't bother checking or confirming. And when it isn't, Mr. Red Brain heads back into the ring!

BrainFishing Tip: If you ask a Closing/Confirming question and you get a flabby, wishy-washy confirmation – don't stop there! Ask the same thing, in a slightly different format, until you get a strong, clear confirmation. If it's important, feel free to confirm it two or even three times, just to be sure. Often asking a Confirming/Closing Question will identify issues that you thought were agreed and clear, and it turns out they weren't. Don't bail out too soon! Be patient and keep fishing.

You: So, I think we're agreed – I'll have the data to you by Wednesday, and the final report will be done by Friday, is that right? (*CC question #1*)
Them: Yeah, that might work. (*Note the lack of commitment!*)
You: It sounded like you'd have plenty of time to finish it. If you have the data Wednesday, will the report be done by Friday? (*CC question #2*)
Them: Yeah, I think that will be okay. (*Again, lack of strong commitment*)
You: Thanks. Can I count 100% on Friday? Can I commit that to the vice-president? (*CC question #3, slightly different*)
Them: Wow, you're serious! Yes, I'll have it by Friday, count on it. (*Done!*)

Don't hesitate to use Confirming/Closing questions liberally, when you need to.

> **EXERCISE #10**

## Confirm and Close

In your next meeting, end each item with a clear Confirming/Closing question, making sure the other party is strong in their confirmation of the agreed outcome. See how this feels, and if it helps bring closure to the issue for all parties.

## FISH STORIES — "Wow..."

A large account salesperson of an international tech company was finishing a very positive meeting with the CFO of a Fortune 100 company:

> **Salesperson:** So, I will sit with your project manager and we will iron out a project plan to accelerate the delivery of the analytics software. Are you good with that? *(CC question #1)*
>
> **Client:** Perfect. Yes, as soon as possible.
>
> **Salesperson:** And I'll send the licencing agreement and contract to your lawyer for immediate review. Can I get that to him first thing in the morning? *(CC question #2)*
>
> **Client:** Yes, that will help speed the process. If it will stall anywhere, it will be in legal, so let's get moving on it.
>
> **Salesperson:** Last point. You said earlier that your team could handle all the implementation issues around deployment and training. Are you still comfortable with that given the scope of what we have been talking about?
> *(CC question #3)*

Client (after a long pause): I'm not sure. If we don't implement on schedule we don't get the return.

Salesperson: Given the size of the investment in this software, how comfortable are you with taking that risk? (*IG question with emotional bait*)

Client: It is a big expenditure....

Salesperson: Can I bring you a proposal to show how we can supplement your team's resources to make sure the software goes in well and on time? (*AP question #1*)

Client: Hmmm, good idea, I'd like to take a look at that.

Salesperson: Is tomorrow okay? (*AP question #2 – a double dose, just to be sure.*)

Client: That would be perfect.

**BrainFishing Analysis:** *Notice how the salesperson ended the meeting with both Confirming/Closing questions and Asking Permission questions to ensure that she and her client were in the same place around the deal. In doing so, she unearthed an emotional interest (around risk) that she was able to address. The client was more comfortable and the salesperson "closed" an additional piece of business. Win-win all around.*

## FISH STORIES — "Teen Angel"

A father and his 14 year-old daughter were talking about a sleepover:

> **Father:** So, you're going to Becky's for her party, and you're sleeping over, right? (*CC question*)
>
> **Daughter:** Uh huh.
>
> **Father:** Great. Are Becky's parents are there all night? (*CC question*)
>
> **Daughter:** Uh huh. See you later, Dad.
>
> **Father:** Just before you go, can I make sure I'm clear on the arrangements? (*AP question*)
>
> **Daughter:** I'm late, so make it quick.
>
> **Father:** Sure. Since Becky's parents are there all night, are you good with me checking in with them later? (*AP question*) It will help me sleep, knowing you're safe.
>
> **Daughter:** No way, I don't want you checking up on me! (*Red Brain response*)
>
> **Father:** What is your concern with me checking in with her parents? (*IG question*)
>
> **Daughter:** It feels like you don't trust me! (*Red Brain attack!*)
>
> **Father:** Since I need to know you're safe and you don't want me calling Becky's parents, what if I dropped by later, to see for myself? (*What If question*)
>
> **Daughter:** No way! I'd rather you called her parents!
>
> **Father:** Okay, that works for me. So I'll call them, not come by, is that right? (*CC question*)
>
> **Daughter:** Yes, just don't come by!

*BrainFishing Analysis: Even in highly resistant situations, Confirming/ Closing questions and Asking Permission questions can help lead to a more positive outcome.*

## Still From Level Three: Magic Words!

Yes, Virginia, there are Magic Words! Magic Words (MW) are simple words which, when used properly, deepen the engagement and thinking of the Blue Brains. Use them sparingly, sprinkle them carefully, and they will help you keep the Blue Brains deeply and constructively engaged. There are initially three words on the Magic Words list – but this is an open-ended list. Identify and add the ones you have found to work well in your world.

### Magic Word #1 – "Specifically"

This is a nice little word. By adding this adverb to a sentence, it deepens the thinking and the focus. And it can be used to ask the same question a second time if the first question didn't get enough traction or response.

Consider this use of "specifically":

### Table 12: Magic Word – "Specifically"

| Magic Words Inserted into Questions: | Impact of this: |
| --- | --- |
| *So, what do you think?* | This is a high-level, open-ended IG question that may only get you a general, high-level response often referred to as "B.S." |
| *What do you think, **specifically**, your role could be in this?* | Here, the Magic Word helps either prevent the B.S. response in the first place, or forces a refined, deeper response to the original question. |

| Magic Words Inserted into Questions: | Impact of this: |
|---|---|
| How, **specifically**, would you implement this? | Ditto. |
| What would you suggest? | If you get a long, weasely response, go to the next question. |
| I'm not sure I'm clear. What, **specifically**, are you suggesting we do next? | Here, the answer must go deeper and clearer because of the focus on "specifically". |

This is a simple, effective word. Used sparingly, it hones the thinking and the outcomes.

### Magic Word #2 – "Might"

No, this is not "might" as in "might makes right". "Might", used properly, is a softening word that makes difficult questions more palatable. It is the spoon full of sugar that makes the medicine go down. Use this in the construction of sensitive questions.

"Might", as a softener, relies mostly on the strongest bait – emotional interests. Using "might" tempers the bluntness of some statements or questions, and leaves the door open for the other parties' input and ideas. People want input and voice – being heard is a strong emotional interest. Using "might", as below, signals that there is room for their views, and invites their thoughts and ideas into the conversation.

Consider these uses of "might":

### Table 13: Magic Word – "Might"

| Instead of this: | Add the Magic Word "Might": |
|---|---|
| I don't think we're using the best approach to this problem. | What are some approaches that **might** work here, in your view? |
| When will you commit to starting the project? | What dates **might** work to get this started? |
| Why won't you agree to participate in the conference? | What **might** be some of your concerns around participating in the conference? |

Notice how using "might" in these questions softens the impact, while still getting directly at the information or issue that needs to be addressed. It also signals an openness to hear the other person's point of view. The statement and questions on the left, while not wrong, run the risk of triggering the Red Brain. A lot depends on how the questions are asked, that's true. By using "might" judiciously, it can give you more latitude in the interaction, and less chance of having to suddenly deal with the Red Brain.

### Magic Word #3 – "And"

This Magic Word is actually the inverse of two other Magic Words – "but" and "however". The problem is that "but" and "however," unfortunately, are words of Dark Magic. They magically conjure the Red Brain, summoning it from wherever it was snoozing or hiding, and inducing anger and resistance almost instantly. In addition, "but" and "however" are what we call "negaters" – they magically reverse or negate whatever it was you just said.

### Table 14: Negating with "But" and "However"

| Negating with "But" and "However": | What they hear: |
| --- | --- |
| That's a good idea, **but** it raises other issues. | That's a lousy idea that won't work! |
| You work hard here, **but** that's not enough. | You're incompetent in other ways, too. |
| The board liked the proposal. **However**, the costs are out of line. | We're not interested because it's too expensive. |

Notice how the main part of the message, *"That's a good idea..."* *"You work hard..."* *"The board liked the proposal..."* gets completely lost, and the focus goes to the opposite and negative inference, *"It won't work..."* *"You're incompetent..."* *"It costs too much..."*

The antidote, the true Magic Word, is the word "and". Simply replace "but" or "however" with the Magic Word "and", and watch the change take place:

### Table 15: Magic Word "And"

| Negating with "But " and "However": | Magic Word " And": |
| --- | --- |
| That's a good idea, **but** it raises other issues. | That's a good idea, **and** it raises a few other issues we'll have to address. |
| You work hard here, **but** that's not enough. | You work hard here, **and** we're also looking for other qualities as well. |
| The board liked the proposal. **However**, the costs are out of line. | The board liked the proposal. **In addition**, they are also concerned about the cost. |

With the Magic Word "and", the first part of the message isn't lost – the second part is simply *added* to the mix as another important aspect. With "but" and "however", the Red Brain jumps in to argue. With the Magic Word "and", the Blue Brain tends to stay engaged past the "and." Which is better for problem solving, in your view?

> **EXERCISE #11**

**Casting Magic Words**

The next time you focus on asking more questions – Information Gathering questions, Problem Solving questions, Reality Changing questions, etc., throw in a few Magic Words:

- Narrow and focus a question or two with "specifically"
- Soften a few questions with a "might"
- Eliminate "but" and "however", and see how adding an "and" can keep the engagement strong

### FISH STORIES — "It's Like, Like...Magic!"

Two directors brought their management teams together to try to resolve a rash of errors that had arisen between the two teams. The one director listened to 10 minutes of complaining from the other director and from his people as well. A lot of finger point-ing, shifting the blame, and generous uses of the words "but" and "however" as the blame-shifting continued.

During a pause while the two teams glared at each, the first director grabbed the flipchart marker and sat back in his chair. "Do you think it *might* be helpful if we put together a list of everything we've been discussing here?" Taking general nodding to be assent, he looked at one of the other team's members – the most negative and vocal – and, standing by the flipchart said: "Bob, dig into that issue you were raising. What *specifically* have we been screwing up in the end-of-day transfers?" Bob gave his answer and the director said: "*And* do you think it would be helpful to look into the backup process as well?" Bob agreed that would be relevant, even though everyone in the room knew it was Bob's team who had control of the backups.

The director wrote the issues on the list and kept moving forward. Within 30 minutes they had 22 issues up on the flipchart and were forming joint teams to address each one.

**BrainFishing Analysis:** *The Magic Words didn't do the work, but they created a space where everyone could breathe a bit and start to open their Blue Brains to solutions rather than accusations. Within a month the teams had 20 of the 22 issues sorted out, and the whole tone and tenor of the relationship had improved noticeably.*

## BrainFishing Summary – From Hobby to Habit

The Practice Guide ends here. As the saying goes, we all reach a time, a point in our lives, when we have to choose to either fish or cut bait. In this case it's to actually give BrainFishing a try, or stay on the dock.

To be clear, we didn't write this little book to advance the research into human behaviour. This isn't a motivational exercise, it isn't a TED talk, and it most certainly isn't the Next Big Idea that will grip North American business theory for decades to come.

It is, and is only, a Practice Guide. A simple set of tools that can help us day in and day out, in our work and personal lives. But it will only be of any value whatsoever if it is, indeed, practised. Put into play. Tried and tested. Applied.

BrainFishing is about behaviour, about acting in a different way to get better outcomes. BrainFishing is simple, but for most of us, it means changing life-long habits. And the only thing we know for sure is this:

### You can't catch a fish until you cast a hook in the water.

So, we leave you with a choice. Keep hunting, keep telling, keep arguing and defending – and put up with more of the same. Keep avoiding, keep ducking, and again, more of the same will come your way. Make peace with the fact you'll be spending most of your time with Red Brains.

Or try fishing. BrainFishing. Ask questions. Choose different types of questions. Dip into Level 2 of your tackle box and acknowledge, then ask more Level 1 questions. Go all the way to Level 3 and ask permission more often. Challenge the other person's reality, gather information and problem solve.

In other words, change the game. Cultivate the intention of making it better for everyone, not just yourself. Above all else, get curious. And when you change the game to make it better for you *and* for other Blue Brains, it will change your life. It may not be "win the lottery" life-changing, but who knows? Let life become one long fishin' derby and see for yourself. We know it will give you far more than you put in.

All of the tools and skills in the tackle box have been captured in a few pages in the BrainFishing Tackle Box section that follows. In addition, we have summarized all the exercises in the Practice Guide in the BrainFishing Worksheets section, for both ease of reference and to give you a simple, clear plan for exactly how you can start applying BrainFishing every day. For those of you ready to jump in and start BrainFishing now, Chapter 3 is purely optional. But for those of you who need something more, some of the brain research for scientific validation, some data, some studies, some additional resources, some verification that all this BrainFishing stuff isn't just, well, fish stories – read on! Chapter Three will give you real food for thought.

We'll try our best to end this silly hunting and fishing metaphor here – we've failed before, however, so no promises. We hope you try some of the tools and skills, we hope that you build your own personal tackle box for constant future use, and we offer you a simple sign you can hang on your door forever....

Good luck. And start BrainFishing!

Chapter Three

# Neuroscience, Habits, and Better BrainFishing

## SECTION A
### Fishing Around in Brain Research

## SECTION B
### Tips for Better Fishing

# SECTION A
# Fishing Around in Brain Research

## 1. What is my brain actually doing when I'm problem-solving?

In developing BrainFishing as a better way to solve problems and achieve more satisfactory outcomes, we looked at research on how the brain works, and particularly how it responds when we ask questions instead of telling. We wanted to know: Why does BrainFishing work better than hunting? How do our brains respond when we ask questions or have them asked of us? We summarize that research briefly here, but there is much to read and understand if this topic particularly interests you.

We will look specifically at the three sections of the brain that are relevant to BrainFishing – the *pre-frontal cortex, the basal ganglia* and the *amygdala*.

The pre-frontal cortex is the section of the brain that we use for serious, contemplative thinking. It is the part of the brain where complex information is processed, thoughtful consideration given and mindful decisions made. In BrainFishing parlance, this is the Blue Brain, the brain that we want to engage, in both ourselves and the other party.

But other parts of the brain fire very quickly.[1] And when under threat – or when we are being *told* what to think – the part of the brain that engages well before the pre-frontal cortex is the amygdala. One of the deeper, older parts of the brain structure – sometimes referred to as part of the "limbic system" – the amygdala is where our fight or flight instincts live. This is part of our *pure* Red Brain. When we feel under threat, we go into a defensive stance; we either fight the threat or flee from it.[2] This response has allowed us to survive for millions of years. Even today, at a time in evolutionary history when we are rarely under specific physical

---

1   It is estimated that the Red Brain fires 4 – 5 times faster than the Blue Brain – so it wins this race every single time!

2   Sometimes we "freeze" first – just lock up. But when we thaw even a bit, it's right back to fight or flight.

threat, it is an immediate and finely honed response to perceived danger, threat or risk.

The other section of the brain that is critical to BrainFishing is the *basal ganglia*, the reptilian brain. The basal ganglia delivers what is termed "automatic memory". This is knowledge we hold that we bring forward without consciously editing or choosing. It is the knowledge that allows us to drive home safely while using our pre-frontal cortex to think about what happened at the office or what is coming up the next day; it holds routines and habits that we act on without consciously thinking about them.

Most relevant to BrainFishing, the basal ganglia is the root of our biases and reflexive opinions: the place from which we pass judgment. When we are "told" something, we instinctively pass judgment whether it is wrong or right. We pass judgment as a defense mechanism. When we pass judgment, we know exactly where we stand. The response is immediate and it is done so that, momentarily, we maintain a degree of certainty in a situation of potential conflict. Judgments help us to eliminate confusion or uncertainty – but they don't help us solve problems or come to win-win solutions. The passing of judgment is a combination of the defense mechanism of the amygdala and the entrenched biases of the basal ganglia. In this way, the basal ganglia is a quieter but equally powerful portion of the Red Brain. And it can get in the way of our truly engaging with another person in complex and challenging situations.

So when we are confronted with a problem or perceived threat, our amygdala and basal ganglia – the Red Brain – are immediately engaged. This reaction is a protective mechanism, like a warning bell. In BrainFishing we are working to quiet both the amygdala and the basal ganglia by inviting the pre-frontal cortex – the Blue Brain – to become fully engaged. This is why it is so important to ask relevant questions and then *shut up and listen* – and listen patiently without judgment or agenda in order to actually understand the other party's point of view. In asking and listening, we are engaging our Blue Brain to engage the other party's Blue Brain in making sound, considered decisions. When the pre-frontal cortex is fully engaged – the Blue Brain – both parties are better able to think, to understand, and to have the contemplative, potential space to understand new, more complex ideas and to formulate collaborative solutions that work to both parties' best interests.

## 2. Why does asking questions make such a big difference? Can't I just "tell" a bit more nicely?

Here is why asking questions makes such a difference: questions invite the other party to think. Questions show respect and they immediately work to highlight and clarify information, biases, assumptions, misaligned definitions or areas of potential confusion. In using questions, we create a problem-solving state of mind, an arena where ideas can be discussed and positive solutions created.

Telling triggers the fight or flight response in the other person by firing the amygdala portion of the brain, among other responses. The impact of being challenged isn't just psychological, it is physiological – the heart beats faster, blood pressure rises, your skin turns pale and your stress level rises quickly.[3] Even "nicer" telling forces the other party to immediately take a position in relation to what we have told them: "That isn't right." "I don't agree with what I am being told." "I don't like the fact that you are telling me what I should think!" Telling fires the amygdala[4] and then the basal ganglia kicks in with our entrenched biases and positions. And we will either take flight from the conversation or dig deeper into our entrenched position and fight.

Daniel Goleman coined the expression "The Amygdala Hijack" to explain this reaction. The amygdala hijacks the whole brain, preventing serious consideration of complex situations and common interest problem solving. Goleman's work on this phenomenon and on emotional intelligence was ground-breaking, a reference source that all BrainFishers should have in their tackle box.[5]

---

3   "Meltdown", Chris Clearfield and Andras Tilcsik, Penguin Canada, 2018
4   This is why "mansplaining", or any kind of 'splaining, really, tends to draw strong, and negative, reactions.
5   "Emotional Intelligence", Daniel Goleman, Bloomsbury, 1995 pp. 59

Goleman outlines how the emotional responses are immediate and overwhelming, and often out of proportion to the actual stimulus because the stimulus has triggered an emotional threat. He notes that emotions "make us pay attention right now—this is urgent—and give us an immediate action plan *without having to think twice* (italics added)". The emotional component evolved in the human brain very early in our development: "Do I eat it, or does it eat me?"[6] The emotional response "can take over the rest of the brain in a millisecond if threatened." An amygdala hijack exhibits three signs: a strong emotional reaction, explosive onset, and post-episode recognition when the reaction was inappropriate.[7]

In order to keep the amygdala in neutral and allow the pre-frontal cortex – the Blue Brain – to engage, we need to establish a trusting, respectful method of engagement. To do this we need to create and hold a space within which all parties feel safe enough to explore, discuss and accept new ideas. And this can realistically only be done through relevant, thoughtful questions and exceptional listening. BrainFishing.

### 3. What psychology is there behind all this BrainFishing stuff?

Psychologists, psychoanalysts, and psychotherapists spend their working lives helping patients to understand how their minds work and how the rich tapestry of past patterns and experience affects their current responses to stimuli. The models and frameworks they use to help patients are wide-reaching and can be highly impactful.

We will draw on one specific model that leads to better BrainFishing. This is the idea of creating a "potential space" within which rich and complex conversations can take place. The term "potential space" was coined originally by Donald Winnicott,[8] a British psychologist who

---

6   "Emotional Intelligence – Stop Amygdala Hijackings" Shell Horowitz
    http://fambizpv.com/articles/values_culture/primal_leadership.html
7   Ibid.
8   "Playing and Reality", Donald W. Winnicott, Routledge, 1971 pp. 107

worked closely with mothers and babies. He believed that it was the role of the mother to create the space, the "potential space", within which her child could safely explore the development of their own identity.

This is exactly what happens when we are BrainFishing, only on an adult level. We are creating – and holding – the space within which it is safe to think, to explore new ideas, to understand each other without judgment. In this "potential space" we can find, through dialogue and the exchange of both common and competing interests, the best solution to the problem, the best path to build a stronger relationship, the best solution for *both* parties.

But to exist in this "potential space" we have to engage our Blue Brains. By asking questions and actively listening, by seeking to understand, and by not passing judgment, we create a safe space for both parties. Questions open up avenues of exploration; they show and hold respect; they create the space where thinking can take place and the best solutions can be generated. We create the space with good questions and patient listening; we create and hold the space by continuously engaging our Blue Brains.

4. *How do I get in the habit of Asking Questions, instead of Telling?*

The key here lies in the question: "How do I get in the *habit* of...?"

First of all, telling is a habit. At some point in our past we have been taught or led to believe – often through the example of a demanding parent or teacher – that conversation between two adults is more about telling than asking: telling others what to do, how to act and behave, what would be a better way to drive, eat, live. Common views of "leadership" see a strong leader as someone who has the answers, who barks instructions or commands, and, well, leads the way. Everyone else follows, period. You get the point. Telling is a learned habit we have taken on at some point in our life. We were encouraged to hunt and never understood why it might better to fish.

Let's look at habits. In his book "The Power of Habit", Charles Duhigg[9] succinctly outlines the steps that occur when a habit is formed and perpetuated:

| **Cue – Response – Reward** |
|---|
| **Cue:** In any action/reaction situation we get a "cue" or stimulus that sends us into a patterned or "habitual" response. The cue is the stimulus – the response is our reaction. |
| **Response:** With habits the response is automatic – *we do it without thinking.* The response has been baked into our nervous system, most likely because on many occasions in the past this response delivered the reward we desired. |
| **Reward:** This is the payoff for any kind of action. Does the response deliver a reward that is repeatable and leads to sustained satisfaction? |

We have hundreds of habits for good reason: they deliver a reward that we desire and they continue to do so. It makes sense that we would repeat habits that deliver. And for most tasks this is a good thing – we take the cue, respond, and reap the reward without having to take the time to be aware of what we are doing or thinking about the next step. Comfortable, efficient, satisfying – who wouldn't want to keep that up?

And there is a second benefit to having habits that is rarely voiced: *we have habits because they save us time.* And they save us time because we don't have to stop and *think*. We don't have to be aware; we don't have to think about how we are responding. Einstein once said: "We have limited decision-making capacity in our brain; we should not waste it on trivial matters."

And that is why we have habits, so that we don't waste our brain power – our Blue Brain power – on trivial matters. Habits are one of the

9    "The Power of Habit", Charles Duhigg, Random House, 2012 pp. 72

greatest examples of the Red Brain in action! But solving important problems or managing critical conflicts is far from a trivial matter. To change those habits – to think! to engage! to plan! – we need to engage our own Blue Brains. If we want better outcomes, better relationships and stronger solutions to problems, we need to think and engage with others, we need to be aware of how we are responding to cues, and we need to plan and prepare, not respond unconsciously or habitually.

If you have waded this far into the BrainFishing pond, most likely it is because you want better outcomes – better "rewards" – to your problem solving, work, or relationship challenges. You want interactions to be more satisfying and to produce stronger solutions and sustainable relationships. And if those rewards are not coming, what you are likely discovering is that the habits you have been using are not working, or at least not working as well as they could.

So what can we do to "change the habit" of automatically telling into the more rewarding habit of asking? In other words, how can we stop hunting as a habit and start BrainFishing?

First, we must be aware of both the situation we are in and the "cues" that are being presented to us. When we are not aware of and watching for the cues, we are more likely to automatically respond with our habit of telling or hunting.

First cue – we are in a discussion. That's it. If we are habitual "tellers", just the fact that there is another person's face and ears in front of us can start us telling. To change that habit, recognize the cue and go to a question – choose to start BrainFishing!

Second cue – someone starts "telling" and it excites our amygdala – we get our back up, we feel the heat rising in our face. These are cues that in the past we may have responded to automatically by telling, by justifying a position, by arguing the facts or premise. The "reward" is feeling like we're right, or "we really told them!" And while that may feel emotionally satisfying for a moment, it rarely leads to a better outcome. So, change the response. Ask a question instead. It gives you time to breathe and calm yourself. Ask another question, such as, "Tell me more about that" – while not an actual question, this brief statement acts exactly like a question to bring out more information and engage the other person's Blue Brain. It also expands and holds the "potential space". If you respond by telling, you are reducing the space and shutting down the potential for deeper understanding and better solutions.

When you know you are entering a particularly challenging situation or conversation, prepare accordingly. Write down two or three relevant questions that you might ask in the situation. But don't stick to them slavishly. This is not a police interrogation. Use your prepared questions as guides to help you ask instead of tell. And when you ask, listen carefully – often the next natural question will fall out of the answers you are hearing.

The best thing about BrainFishing is that we can do it in *every* conversation we enter into. We are building a new habit and we have the opportunity every day in every conversation to practice. Ask. Listen. Ask again. Be aware of the questions you are asking and how you are responding – and how the other person is responding. Be aware of the exact moment when you want to start telling; take a breath and instead of telling, ask a question and shut up and listen. And most importantly, be aware of the different kinds of responses, and outcomes, you get. When the outcomes get better, you'll start BrainFishing more and more!

5. **I think I'm too set in my ways to change – can my brain really learn to do this?**

We all grew up hearing the expression, "you can't teach an old dog new tricks". Setting aside our resentment at being called dogs, and old ones at that, the expression is actually dead wrong.

The research on this couldn't be clearer – young and old dogs alike can not only learn new skills, new abilities, new "tricks", our brains actually re-work and re-wire themselves to make that happen. In science, it is called "neuroplasticity," which essentially means that based on what we focus on and practice doing in this life, our brains adapt and get good at it. At any age at all.

Some examples.

- In many experiments, mental training increases brain weight by 5% in the cerebral cortex of animals, and up to a 9% increase can be seen in areas of the brain that the training directly stimulated.[10]

- Trained and stimulated neurons develop 25% more branches and increase their size, the number of connections per neuron, and their blood supply.

- Michael Merzenich, a leading neurologist and one of the world's most respected researchers on brain plasticity, says, "The cerebral cortex is actually selectively refining its processing capacities to fit each task at hand." He claims that we can change the structure of the brain itself while increasing its capacity to learn.[11]

These are not just theoretical claims. Read Norman Doidge's books[12] to read stories of people returning from crippling strokes and significant brain damage to a more normal life – based on their brain re-learning important skills by utilizing undamaged parts of itself. Doidge coined the phrase, "What wires together, fires together." This means that when we repeatedly practice a new skill, our brain creates new pathways of neurons that solidify these new habits and skills. Because of this, they become easier and easier to access and use.

In this context, there is no doubt that anyone, with practice and focus, can learn the skill of asking effective questions. And doing so will likely also strengthen and develop your capacity for listening, learning and empathizing, to boot.

---

10  "The Brain That Changes Itself", Norman Doidge, M.D., Penguin Books, 2007, pp. 43
11  Ibid., pp. 47
12  Also read "The Brain's Way of Healing: Remarkable Discoveries and Recoveries from the Frontiers of Neuroplasticity", Viking Penguin, 2015

### 6. *This Red Brain/Blue Brain stuff seems stupid – is this actually how the brain works?*

In a word, yes – with a few caveats. There is a distinction between how the brain works, and how the mind works. The brain is a physical organ with a structure that has evolved over millions of years. It evolved in a particular order, starting with the reptilian brain (basal ganglia), followed by the limbic system (paleo-mammalian complex, including the amygdala), and most recently by the pre-frontal cortex (neo-mammalian complex).

These brain parts, such as the amygdala and the rest of the limbic system, the basal ganglia, the pre-frontal cortex, etc., have been mapped to a large degree, and their functions documented. The science on this is pretty good.[13]

Much of BrainFishing, however, is based on how the *mind* works, on patterns of thinking, on how the mind makes decisions and operates. For sake of simplicity, we have mapped the Red Brain to the basal ganglia and the limbic system, and the Blue Brain to the pre-frontal cortex. At a mid-level of detail, this overlay maps very well.

So, how the mind works has also been studied extensively, independent of the underlying brain structures. There are at least two excellent and readable sources for understanding, in more depth, how the mind works.

First, Daniel Kahneman is a psychologist who has won the Nobel Prize (in economics!) for his work in uncovering how the mind works. He describes it most simply as having two "systems", System One and System Two. System One is, essentially, the Red Brain – the part of the brain that operates automatically, scanning our environment for threats and treats, and helping us stay safe. System Two is the Blue Brain, the conscious thinking part of the brain, which can solve complex problems one step at a time. For greater detail on how the mind works well beyond our simplified version of Red Brain/Blue Brain, see his excellent book, "Thinking, Fast and Slow".[14]

---

13  Strategy + Business, Summer 2006 Issue 43, David Rock and Jeffrey Schwartz, https://www.strategy-business.com/article/06207?gko=6da0a

14  Kahneman, Daniel, "Thinking, Fast and Slow", Anchor Canada, 2013

If you want more of these colourful metaphors for how the mind works, Johnathan Haidt published an equally fine book on this subject, "The Happiness Hypothesis".[15] The metaphor he employs is that of the elephant and the rider. In essence, the Red Brain (or System One) is the elephant, a large and strong beast with strong views on where it is going in the forest as it hunts for food, water and safety. The rider is the Blue Brain (or System Two), the conscious guide who can steer the elephant at times, but in moments of fear and threat, the elephant will do what it needs to do, frequently ignoring the rider. When fight or flight hits, the rider, i.e. the Blue Brain, is simply ignored, and is just along for the ride. The most powerful element of Haidt's elephant metaphor is the relationship in terms of size and power between the elephant and the rider. The elephant is huge and physically powerful; the rider is much smaller and much weaker – it is only through the use of intelligence and awareness that the rider is able to direct the more powerful elephant. We think this is a telling metaphor for the difference between the Red Brain – powerful, animalistic, blunt – and the Blue Brain – subtle, complex, nuanced.

BrainFishing is a simple, direct and useful metaphor that applies the learnings of both Kahneman's and Haidt's books, and many more on the topic. The dominant metaphors in both books follow the same pattern we have outlined in BrainFishing. So, the short answer is yes, the brain and the mind have a strong tendency to behave this way. If you want more depth, dig in – these two books are an excellent place to start. But remember, BrainFishing is about actually fishing for Blue Brains – not just reading about fishing from your easy chair. Reading is good – but not in lieu of actually engaging with the Blue Brains all around you.

15  Haidt, Jonathan , "The Happiness Hypothesis", Basic Books, 2006

## SECTION B
## Tips for Better Fishing

~~~~~~~~~~~~~~~~~~~~~~~~~~~

**7.  How do I break my habit of wanting to give them the "right" answer off the top?**

This is the next level to the "habit" issue raised in Question #4 above. First, how do I change my habit from telling to asking? Second, how do I break my habit of giving them the "right" answer – or frankly, any answer at all.

For this we take you back to the Duhigg model outlined above. We need to divorce ourselves from the belief that we have the "right" answer. If we judgmentally tell the other party the "right" answer, we are only going to trigger their amygdala and launch them into a fight or flight response.

In any problem solving situation, the "best" outcome rarely comes solely from ourselves or the other party, but rather from the dialogue that takes place between us. We work *together* to understand and meet both parties' interests and both parties contribute to a better and more sustainable solution.

To change the habit of wanting to give them the right answer, start by changing the "reward" you are looking for. In other words, change your intention. Change your intention from "being right" to "being right together". With this as your intention, your response will be to ask questions and to engage the other party's Blue Brain, to seek a deeper understanding and an authentic, win-win solution.

**8.  How do I think of the "right" questions?**

There is no such thing as the "right" question. First, we need to shift our thinking from "right" questions to "relevant" questions or relevant areas of questioning. Second, we need to think about the type of question we are asking, as we discuss in the tackle box section of Chapter Two.

All this points to how well we prepare when attempting to solve a problem. Good preparation is key to good interactions and satisfying outcomes. It is also critical to changing our habit pattern from hunting to fishing, from telling to asking. So before we engage with another party, we prepare a set of relevant, open-ended questions. This is our bait. To be attractive to the other party, the questions need to be focused on the topics that are relevant to the problem we are solving, and relevant to that other Blue Brain. The questions also need to address both factual and emotional issues that we anticipate will come up in the conversation. Preparing our questions ahead of time also allows us to consider how and when we can raise important topics in a manner that will not send the other party back into their Red Brain.

So, our questions need to be focused into areas that are both important and relevant to the other party, areas related to content, to good process, or to emotions. This allows us to open the conversation in a constructive way. Even more importantly, the preparation of relevant, appropriate questions encourages us to… listen!

And to listen with full empathy and the intention to understand. To listen with genuine curiosity. If your intention is to ask and listen with *genuine curiosity*, you'll hear answers and information that will lead you to the *next* relevant question – and that will be the "right" question because it will be connected to the thoughts and feelings of the other person and to the situation and issues that you are both engaged in thinking about. Remember, a good question is an invitation to think. To think is to engage our Blue Brains and work together to find the best common-interest solutions.

9. *How do I come up with good follow-up questions in my preparation when I don't know where the conversation might be going?*

If you combine a good set of relevant questions with strong listening skills and genuine curiosity, then the follow up questions will come naturally out of the conversation, particularly if you follow the good fishing practice of seeking "to understand before making yourself understood."[16]

With a short list of prepared, relevant questions, you can allow any subject that comes up to follow its full course with good listening and follow up questions. You can then come back to the next most relevant question on your list. Remember, we are BrainFishing to engage the Blue Brain and we are engaging the Blue Brain to facilitate collaborative thinking and an interest-based solution. We are *not* conducting a police interrogation. You don't have to drain your entire list of prepared questions by the end of the conversation as long as both parties are engaged and discovering relevant information and opinions, as long as you are moving together toward a win-win solution. Ask the relevant questions at the right time as needed. Then listen and think and let the Blue Brains flourish!

### 10. Why can I only think of better things to say long after the conversation is over?

Ah, the infamous *Esprit de l'escalier*. That winning comeback that comes to us after the conversation is over and everyone has departed. "If I had only said this…I would have won the argument. Why didn't I think of that at the time?!" This experience exposes two ideas we have explored above.

First, your intention should never be to "win the argument". Your intention should be to win together, not deliver a winning blow. When you change the intention from winning to listening and understanding, you will rarely be in an argument that ends with a winner and a loser. You won't need that zinger after all!

Second, this after-meeting regret usually arises because you have been looking for the wrong outcome. If your intention is to create a win-win situation then the opportunity to "zing" someone is never part of the interaction.

---

16  Covey, Stephen Stephen, "The 7 Habits of Highly Effective People", Simon & Schuster, 1989

The after-meeting regret we should be watching for is when we leave an issue unresolved with everyone's interests unmet. In other words, when we have not finished or closed the conversation completely. The last question that we should ask in any problem-solving situation is some form of: *"What else should we be discussing that we might have missed?"* This allows the potential space to remain open, for final thoughts to lead toward a positive conclusion, for other relevant issues to arise, and for both parties – using their full Blue Brain capabilities – to ensure that all their important needs have been addressed.

## 11. *In a situation where I need to convey information or a point-of-view on an issue, how do I shift from asking to telling and back again?*

There are times you will want to tell and times you will need to tell, especially when you are expected to provide relevant expertise or experience to the discussion.

But never forget that anything you tell may send the other person running for their Red Brain, to resist, to fight or flee, to argue and return to an entrenched position. Remember, at all times it is critical to keep the Blue Brain engaged and to hold the "potential space" for further exploration and areas of agreement.

As a valuable rule, remember that any dose of telling should be short, and followed by a question[17], such as:

- *"Here is the information you requested. (Convey the information, followed by...) How will that impact what we are trying to do? If what I just said makes sense, where does it fit with what you are thinking?"*
- *"Here is what the client told us. (Convey the information, followed by...) How valuable is that?"*

17  This is the Statement-to-Question from the tackle box, page 90.

- *"The data doesn't look good, here it is. (Convey the information, followed by...) What other information would help us here? In addition to what I just covered, what could you add to that? What else could expand our thinking here?"*

Questions like these keep the Blue Brain engaged and hold the "potential space" for further exploration. The other person hears the tell, but immediately has their Blue Brain engaged by the question. Rather than fighting or fleeing, the Blue Brain instead considers the relevance or value of that information to the overall solution.

In situations where both parties are clearly in their Blue Brains and are collaboratively problem solving it may be more appropriate to tell a bit more, but make sure telling doesn't dominate the conversation. Continue to check in as you go along with questions such as the examples above. Stay aware of any shift on the part of the other party where they may be heading back into their Red Brain.

Remember what was outlined in the tackle box – if you get resistance to what you are saying, ask the other party's permission to share relevant information – use an Asking Permission question. Once the permission is granted, share the information or point-of-view in a brief and succinct way, then follow up with a question, a Statement-to-Question. By granting permission, they are more likely to listen and keep their Blue Brain engaged.

### 12. Why should I be the one doing all the asking and listening? It isn't fair!

Yes!!! You are right! It isn't fair! We agree. And so what? Ask yourself this question: *"Do I want to spend my life complaining about fairness, or do I want to be successful and effective, and build better relationships?"* If you choose complaining, all the best and good luck. If you want to be effective, take the lead on asking and listening. Own it. Engage the Blue Brains, theirs *and* yours. Hold the potential space so the conversation can be meaningful and productive. The rewards are much greater than the complaints.

### 13. So if I change, what will make them change?

*"Is there one word which may serve as a rule of practice all one's life?"*
The Master said, *"Is not reciprocity such a word?"*

*Confucius, The Analects, Book 15, Chapter 23*

This is really important. There is a powerful principle at play here, often called the Law of Reciprocity. It turns out that humans are hard-wired to reciprocate, to give back to others what they have been given. But this is a tricky law.

For example, if I give you disrespect, there is no doubt that you will likely give me disrespect back – in spades! If I give you anger and aggression, I am likely to get the same, or greater, back. I may get passive aggression back for my overt aggression, but I'll get the same back.

And the reverse is also true – if I give you respect, you will feel some pressure to be respectful back. If I ask questions and hear you out, you feel some need or desire to return the favour. Notice the phrase we use – "return the favour". Many times we feel that we must return favours – this is the Law of Reciprocity at work.

This means that the more we approach people with curiosity and respect, the more they will return that favour. The more we try and meet their interests (as well as ours), the more they will likely do the same. This will not remain a one-sided exercise for long.

That said, there are certainly a few people in this life that will not reciprocate anything positive (but will likely escalate and reciprocate the negative). For most people, your making the First Shift will cause the Second Shift in them. For a very, very few, nothing will. Watch for these few, and be aware that reciprocity will simply not be effective with them.

For information on the role of reciprocity, you can find more in-depth research and treatment of this idea in:

- *A Cooperative Species – Human Reciprocity and its Evolution*, Samuel Bowles and Herbert Gintis, Princeton Press, 2011
- *Influence: The Psychology of Persuasion*, Robert Cialdini, HarperCollins, 1993
- *The Happiness Hypothesis*, Jonathan Haidt, Basic Books, 2006

From a neurochemical point of view, reciprocity seems to be based on what are called "mirror neurons", a type of neuron in the brain that is linked to experiencing the same feelings that we see in another person. It is often referred to as the source of empathy in humans. While this area of science is still being developed, there seems to be consensus that mirror neurons play a key role in the processes we have covered in this Practice Guide. An outstanding resource on the topic of mirror neurons is:

- *New Frontiers in Mirror Neurons Research*, Pier Francesco Ferrari (Editor), Giacomo Rizzolatti, Oxford University Press, 2015

## 14. What do I do when I think I am not getting a truthful answer to my questions? Or when I sense the other person has a "hidden agenda"?

When you are in any situation where you question the authenticity or intention of what you are being told, follow this pattern: Listen carefully, *acknowledge* what you're hearing, and ask *another* question that goes even deeper into the interests, yours or theirs.

Here are examples of the pattern:

- **Truthfulness issue:** "I hear what you're saying, I'm just not sure that it makes sense to me. What information confirms what you're telling me?"
- **Hidden Agenda issue:** "I'm a bit confused, you had indicated X was important, and it seemed we addressed that. What am I missing?"

Follow the pattern: listen, acknowledge, ask a question that goes deeper – but find your own language. There is a danger that your own amygdala will start to fire and you will – with indignation – slip into a fight or flight stance. Take a breath and be patient. Don't lose your genuine curiosity as you are exploring the issue. There is always the outside chance you may be wrong in your interpretation of what they are doing or that you have misunderstood a point they are making – seek to understand...ask a question...shut up...listen...keep BrainFishing...

**15. What do I do when someone becomes suspicious because I am doing so much asking and listening and not telling?**

This will rarely happen if you are genuinely asking and listening and doing an *appropriate* amount of telling. There is a balance to be struck here. A rule of thumb is that we should be talking 30 – 40% of the time and no more. A 70/30% or 60/40% ratio of them talking to us talking will keep the balance in a reasonable range.

In addition, asking and listening are empathetic, respectful ways to converse; when approached this way, most people will be focused on the content of issues you are discussing and their own thoughts about them, particularly as they apply to how their interests are, or are not, being met. If they pass a judgment, it will most likely be a positive one – that you are a thoughtful, considerate person interested in them and the best solution to solving the problem.

**16. If intention is so important, how should I convey it in these conversations? Do I tell them? If so, how?**

First, to convey our intentions, we need to first be clear on our intentions and the reasons for them.

Our baseline intention should be to work together to come to an agreement or solution that meets as many of both parties' interests as possible. This is a process intention, i.e. *how* we will work together.

We can convey this intention by simply agreeing at the beginning of the discussion how we will work together. We can do this by asking good process-focused questions right from the start:

- *"How can we approach this to make sure both our interests are being identified and met?"*
- *"What should the agenda for that look like?"*
- *"What do you see as our common interests?"*
- *"Where do you think we should start?"*

If you express an intention to work together toward a solution that meets both your interests, then all other content and emotion-based issues can be addressed within that framework – you will have engaged the other party's Blue Brain in working out a fair and transparent process – the first and essential step towards successful BrainFishing!

### 17. What if my intention is not win-win?

You know what they say at the fishing lodge: *"You can fool all of the fish some of the time, some of the fish all of the time, but you can't fool all of the fish all of the time."*

You can't fake a win-win intention. You will be found out, and once others see you are only there for your own interests, not for both yours and theirs, all you will ever see is their Red Brain. It's a very short-term strategy. You may score some wins – for yourself – but over time it will fail far more than it succeeds. And what is worse, you will always be hiding your real intentions. People sense these things, and they simply won't trust you. But if you want to "fish" that way – basically hunting in hip waders – well, all we can say is, "Good luck with that!"

## 18. *What if the other party's intention is clearly not win-win?*

This is the scenario we are always looking out for, whether we relish or dread the challenge. We find ourselves in a situation where the other party is purely hunting. They have no interest in your interests. By bullying, threatening, withholding information, ignoring your concerns, they are determined every time to win – and to see that you lose. This is usually fairly evident from the moment they start talking.

So how do we engage? Do we reach for our rifle and start firing back? Or do we take a breath, see the situation for what it is, and go even deeper into the other party's interests?

It helps to understand that there are fundamentally three approaches[18] or strategies that, as individuals, we can take to achieve what we need:

1. **Power** – we can use our advantages of position and better resources (money, time, authority) to overpower the other person; in other words, to put them and keep them in the place we want them. We win – they lose. Pure hunting.

2. **Rights** – we can appeal to rights granted to us by contracts, laws or the judicial system. Rights also bring a focus on "we win" and "they lose". Or maybe more accurately, "we are right" and "they are wrong".

3. **Interests** – we can work with the other party to ensure that both of our interests are being met. This is BrainFishing. More productive. More satisfying. Better outcomes all around.

When you are facing an individual who only knows or only chooses to work from a Power or Rights position – a position where they believe they only win if you lose – it can be very challenging to stay engaged. Our emotional reaction can be to follow our Red Brain instinct and start to fight or take flight.

---

18   For an in-depth understanding of the three approaches, see "The Conflict Resolution Toolbox", Gary T Furlong, Chapter 7 pg. 109, Wiley and Sons, 2005

Yet, experience shows that finding a way to work from a position of Interests rather than from Rights or Power produces better results and more satisfying relationships. The challenge we are faced with is how to get from here – where we are being hunted – to there, where everyone is engaged and working toward common interests. This is the greatest BrainFishing challenge!

If someone comes at you with a Power-based approach, there are strategies you can use to turn this back to engaged problem solving:

- Most importantly, don't give them what they want. If they win by using Power or Rights, it's all you'll ever see. Most people continue to use Power because they get rewarded for it – and it becomes their go-to habit. What you permit, you promote.

- In some cases, you will also need to go briefly to Power or Rights – just long enough to send the message to them that they will not get what they want this way. Then, immediately – immediately! – go back to BrainFishing – ask questions about what's important to them, what they need, why they want it, etc. This "looping back" to Interests is a BrainFishing specialty.

- Remember, they are only using Rights and Power to try and get their Interests met. When they see that they can get their Interests met in a different way, in a BrainFishing way, they will be much more likely go there. Particularly if you have shown them that a Power or Rights move will not work.

So, keep dangling bait, keep engaging them around their own interests, that make it hard for them to refuse – good open-ended questions are the tastiest morsels – and in doing so entice their Blue Brains to come out and play. Better outcomes. More emotionally satisfying. Win-win all around. BrainFishing.

# The BrainFishing
# Tackle Box

This chapter summarizes the guts of this Practice Guide, the essence of BrainFishing. We pointed you, the budding BrainFisher, to the following:

## 1. Two Shifts and Intention

- The First Shift is ours – the shift from telling to asking good questions.

- This First Shift leads directly to the Second Shift which is theirs – the shift from their Red Brain to their Blue Brain.

- Both shifts have to be wrapped in an intention to create a win-win outcome that benefits both of us. Intention is what makes BrainFishing a successful, long-term strategy.

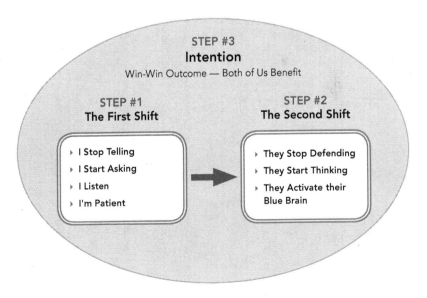

2. **Lesson 1: Basic BrainFishing Equipment.**

   - Ask Questions. Stop Telling. Ask Questions.

   - Be truly curious, not judgmental.

   - Ask open questions (In the Third Tray there are a couple useful closed questions, but stay with open almost all the time.)

3. **Lesson 2: Baiting the Hook , Casting and Reeling.**

   - **Baiting the hook is critical, and there are three kinds of interests we can use as bait:**
     - ▸ Result Interests
     - ▸ Process Interests
     - ▸ Emotional or Psychological Interests

   - **Casting and Reeling: Questioning and Listening**
     - ▸ Casting: Ask open questions baited with interests into the conversation. These questions awaken the Blue Brain in everyone.
     - ▸ Reeling: Listening sets the hook and draws the Blue Brain toward effective engagement and problem solving. Listening happens at three Levels:
       1. Level One: Surface listening – lights on, but nobody home
       2. Level Two: Listening to argue
       3. Level Three: Insight – listening to understand

4. **Lesson 3: Filling Your Tackle Box. This was a big one:**

A) **Level One: First Tray** – Open Questions:
   - Information Gathering questions (IG)
   - Problem Solving questions (PS)
   - Reality Changing questions (RC)
     ▸ "What If"... RC questions (WI)
   - Statement-to-Question (STQ)

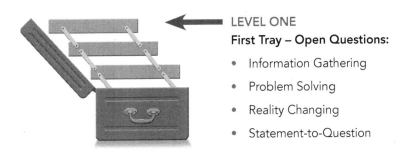

**LEVEL ONE**
**First Tray – Open Questions:**
   - Information Gathering
   - Problem Solving
   - Reality Changing
   - Statement-to-Question

B) **Level Two: Second Tray** – Acknowledging/Empathy Statements (AE)
   - Acknowledging, validating, empathizing

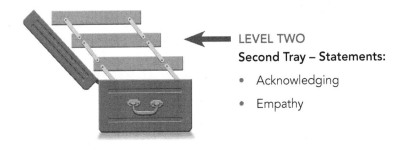

**LEVEL TWO**
**Second Tray – Statements:**
   - Acknowledging
   - Empathy

**C) Level Three: Third Tray** – Closed Questions and Magic Words
- Ask Permission questions (AP)
- Confirming/Closing questions (CC)
- Magic Words (MW):
    ▸ "Specifically…"
    ▸ "Might…"
    ▸ "And…"

**LEVEL THREE**

**Third Tray – MiscellaneousTools:**
- Asking Permission Questions
- Confirming/Closing Questions
- Magic Words

# BrainFishing Worksheets

**Curiosity and Open Questions**

Judgment and Curiosity Exercise

- **Judgment:** The next time you are talking to someone about anything, try this – tell them at least twice that they are wrong. Note their reaction:

  _____

  _____

  _____

- **Curiosity:** Shift to being genuinely curious. Ask questions to understand, to clarify. Be really interested. Thank them for what you just learned. Note their reaction:

  _____

  _____

  _____

### Open and Closed Question Exercise

- **Closed Questions:** In your next conversation, ask them a string of deliberately closed questions such as: *"Did you...? Aren't you...? Couldn't you have...? Don't you agree that...?"* Note carefully what happens:

  _____

  _____

  _____

  _____

- **Open Questions:** After their Red Brain is fully apparent, switch to open questions: *"What do you think about...? Tell me more about.... How might we...? What other ideas do you have about....?"* Note how long it takes for their Blue Brain to come out and play and how quickly they calm down, start thinking again, relax, and engage.

  _____

  _____

  _____

  _____

## ➤ EXERCISE #2

**Questions and the Three Types of Interests**

Baiting the Hook and Casting Exercise:
1. **Result Questions:**

- Think of a situation you need to address. Write three questions that ask the other person about the results they want, what other outcomes might work, and what options they see for solving the situation.

1. _____

2. _____

3. _____

2. **Process Questions:**

- Think about the process, structure, or framework – the context that this situation is taking place in. Write three questions that get their thoughts on how fair the process is, how decisions will be made, what other information would be helpful, what they like about the context or framework they're in.

1. _____

2. _____

3. _____

## 3. Emotion Questions:

- Think about how they might be feeling. Write three questions that focus on how they feel, what they see as important, how they feel they've been treated, what they see as respectful in the situation.

1. _____

2. _____

3. _____

Where did each type of question direct or focus the conversation?

_____

_____

_____

➤ EXERCISE #3

**Three Levels of Listening**

After asking some questions based on the three types of interests, go directly to Level Three Listening:

**Level Three: Insight – Listening to Understand**

- Questions that clarify:

_____

_____

- Paraphrase/summarize what they've said, capture what that sounded like:

_____

_____

_____

- Acknowledge what you heard (without agreeing):

_____

_____

_____

➤ **EXERCISE #4**

## Information Gathering Questions

Focus deliberately on asking Information Gathering (IG) questions. Write out some questions that would engage the other person in thinking about and giving you good information in the situation. Some of these IG questions might be:

_____

_____

_____

> **EXERCISE #5**

## Problem Solving Questions

Build on the last Information Gathering exercise. After asking one or two IG questions, follow up with one or two Problem Solving (PS) questions. Some of these PS questions might be:

_____

_____

_____

> **EXERCISE #6**

## Acknowledging/Empathy Statements

Identify a number of Acknowledging/Empathy (AE) statements that work for you:

_____

_____

_____

> **EXERCISE #7**

## Changing Reality with Reality Changing Questions

Practicing with Reality Changing (RC) questions requires more thought and preparation than with Information Gathering or Problem Solving questions. Follow this process to create effective Reality Changing questions, and practice it a few times:

## How to Chart Reality Changing Questions:

| **#1:** Identify what you want to convey, or what you want them to have to consider and think about. Be specific: | **#2:** Identify *their* interests – what impacts them, what do they want, what are they afraid of around this issue: |
| --- | --- |
|  |  |

**#3:** Based on the above information, prepare questions that you can ask that will cause them to see reality differently, see consequences they have been ignoring, or see the problem from a different angle:

## How to Chart Reality Changing Questions:

**#1:** Identify what you want to convey, or what you want them to have to consider and think about. Be specific:

**#2:** Identify *their* interests – what impacts them, what do they want, what are they afraid of around this issue:

**#3:** Based on the above information, prepare questions that you can ask that will cause them to see reality differently, see consequences they have been ignoring, or see the problem from a different angle:

## ➤ EXERCISE #8

### Changing More Reality With What If Questions

Try the same exercise as above, but this time practice by focusing the questions in box #3 on What If (WI) questions:

**How to Chart Reality Changing "What If" Questions:**

| #1: Identify what you want to convey, or what you want them to have to consider and think about. Be specific: | #2: Identify *their* interests – what impacts them, what do they want, what are they afraid of around this issue: |
|---|---|
| | |

#3: Based on the above information, prepare three What If questions that you can ask that will cause them to see reality differently, see consequences they have been ignoring, see the problem from a different angle:

After test-driving a few Reality Changing and/or What If questions, answer the following:

1. What happened when you asked a Reality Changing or a What If question?

_____

_____

_____

2. What signs did you see of them having to think, or re-think, the situation (pausing to consider, looking up and away for a moment, starting and stopping in their response, some new uncertainty, or acknowledging the new focus you brought to the situation)?

_____

_____

_____

> **EXERCISE #9**

## Ask Permission Questions

For the next week, try asking permission with a good Asking Permission (AP) question before just leaping ahead with your next idea. Capture the ones you found to work well:

_____

_____

_____

> **EXERCISE #10**

## Confirm and Close

In your next meeting, end each item with a clear Confirming/Closing (CC) question, making sure the other party is strong in their confirmation of the agreed outcome. Capture the ones you found to work well:

_____

_____

_____

_____

> **EXERCISE #11**

## Casting Magic Words

The next time you focus on asking more questions – Information Gathering questions, Problem Solving questions, Reality Changing questions, etc., throw in a few Magic Words (MW). Capture the ones you found to work well:

_____

_____

_____

_____

## Journal of Questions

Consider starting a journal of questions that you've found to be effective:

**Information Gathering questions that worked well:**

_____

_____

_____

**Problem Solving questions that worked well:**

_____

_____

_____

**Reality Changing questions that worked well:**

_____

_____

_____

_____

**What If questions that worked well:**

_____

_____

_____

_____

_____

**Acknowledging/Empathy statements I found that worked for me:**

_____

_____

_____

_____

**Magic Words that have worked:**

_____

_____

_____

_____

_____

And if you want more BrainFishing, check out:

**brainfishing.ca**

# The Authors

JIM HARRISON has over 30 years of experience in consulting, training, and executive coaching with experience in financial services, technology, health care, human resources and public service. He has worked for companies and public services organizations in more than 25 countries including IBM, Accenture, Deloitte, KPMG, AGFA, Fuji, CIBC, TD-Canada Trust, HSBC, Deutsche Bank, the Government of Alberta, the Ontario Ministry of the Attorney General and many others.

Jim specializes in sales and negotiation skills, strategic planning, partnering, analytics, and executive coaching. In addition, he teaches two programs at the Queen's University Industrial Relations Centre in Business Strategy for HR professionals and HR Metrics and Analytics.

Jim received his Bachelor of Science in Finance from Florida State University and a Master's Degree in English from the University of California, Irvine. He is a published author and playwright, and a former Canadian Junior and Ontario Amateur Golf Champion.

GARY T FURLONG has extensive experience in mediation, alternative dispute resolution, negotiation, and conflict resolution. Gary is past president of the ADR Institute of Ontario, is a Chartered Mediator (C. Med.) and holds his Master of Laws (ADR) from Osgoode Hall Law School. As a mediator of 25 years, Gary has worked in the areas of personal injury, employment, labour, construction, insurance, and specializes in intervening in difficult organizational and workplace disputes.

Gary has delivered conflict management training for judges, police officers and firefighters, as well as thousands of managers and union leaders across Canada and the United States. Gary teaches negotiation skills at the Queen's University Industrial Relations Centre, and was awarded the McGowan Award of Excellence in ADR by the ADR Institute of Canada.

Gary is a principal with Agree Dispute Resolution, and is a graduate of Stanford University in California.

## Other books by Gary T Furlong:

*The Conflict Resolution Toolbox*, Gary T Furlong, Wiley and Sons Canada, 2005

*The Sports Playbook: Building Teams That Outperform, Year after Year*,
   Joshua Gordon, Gary T Furlong, Ken Pendleton, Routledge, New York, 2018

*The Construction Dispute Resolution Handbook*, Gary T Furlong, Robert Silver,
   LexisNexis Canada, 2004